Praise for Reachi

I am sure readers will have a hard time putting this book down. The adventures of this wonderful couple will make them envious. I am very glad to have been a part of them.

—Dr. Charles W. (Bill) Gay, Former U.S. Fulbright Scholar
Japan and Former Director American Language Institute,
University of Southern California, Los Angeles, California.

I am heartened by this timely reminder that we are all capable of reaching out to our neighbors. This book captivates with detailed stories of what it takes to offer oneself as a cultural ambassador. I especially resonate with the adventures in Tokyo, as I knew them during that foundational time for bringing intercultural awareness and learning center stage.

—Sheila Ramsey, Ph.D., Co-founder-Personal Leadership Seminars,
LLC and our former inter-cultural trainer, Tokyo, Japan.

At a time when the West seems to be regressing into more nationalistic views of the world, 'Reaching Across Borders' offers a relevant and refreshing reminder of the joy and enlightenment derived from cross-cultural experience.

—Michael E. Rudder, Ph.D. Former Regional English Language
Officer (RELO), U.S. Department of State, Jakarta, Indonesia.

Jeff and Shelly are the people I've admired most in my life. They truly are cultural ambassadors and years ago opened my young eyes and mind to the world. This book will provide you with insights on how to overcome cultural barriers in your daily life, especially when living abroad, and how to show respect and empathy toward other cultures. If we all had the compassion and international goodwill Jeff and Shelly do, the world would definitely be a better place!

—Nanako Kumamoto, Secretary General of the Japanese
Association in Thailand, Bangkok, Thailand. Former
American Field Service exchange student to the U.S.

A book like 'Reaching Across Borders' is so urgently needed at this time if we are to eliminate the gulf between cultures and more importantly, if we are to have any humanity. I'm so glad Jeff has taken on this rejection of isolationism to help people value each other more regardless of their race, nationality, ethnicity, culture, country of origin, class, and more. We are so fortunate to have also been the beneficiary of his dedicated service to the Thai immigrant community in Los Angeles. His quest to unite—not divide—is the first step to conquering people's misplaced fear of 'the other', and to really seeing each other, thereby creating real and everlasting world peace.

—Chanchanit (Chancee) Martorell, Executive Director, Thai Community Development Center, Los Angeles, California.

Jeff Kealing's acute observations and first-hand experience living in at least five different parts of the world will be eye opening for readers who interact with different cultures, either while abroad or within their own countries. The lessons go beyond the five sites - each with their own unique cultures - that Jeff and Shelly have experienced and shared in this book. These 'lessons' are applicable not only for their fellow citizens in the U.S. but also for the citizens of the world.

—Pandu Harimurti, Senior Health Specialist, The World Bank Jakarta and graduate of the International Public Policy and Management Program (IPPAM), University of Southern California, Los Angeles

Reaching Across Borders

How We Became American
Cultural Ambassadors
—And How You Can, Too

Reaching Across Borders

How We Became American Cultural Ambassadors
—And How You Can, Too

By Jeffrey Kealing, Ph.D

William Charles

For permission requests, please address
William Charles Press
7300 W. Joy Road
Dexter, MI 48130

Published 2019 by William Charles Press
Printed in the United States of America

21 20 19   1 2 3 4
ISBN 978-1-943290-91-8

Library of Congress Control Number: 2018966607

"To Barbara and Richard Westebbe, members of the greatest generation, who paved the way...."

—TABLE OF CONTENTS—

Prologue: In Appreciation of America's International Visionaries

After the devastation of two world wars, the 20th-century world was long overdue to find new ways for nations to communicate and co-exist. Some initiatives emerged even before the Second World War had drawn to a close. In 1944, the United States-led Bretton Woods Conference resulted in the creation of the World Bank and the International Monetary Fund.[1] Soon after, the U.S. played a leading role in the negotiations to establish the United Nations that took place in San Francisco. As its main funder from the start, the U.S. has always had an oversized impact on the U.N.[2]

Besides these very visible efforts to restore order and create liberal democratic institutions in Western Europe and Japan, there were other, quieter changes occurring that helped to nurture the development of peace and prosperity. New international exchange programs in the mid–20th century helped foster the personal relationships needed to rebuild devastated countries during that era of U.S. leadership.

A little-known American idealist pioneered these goodwill programs. Even back in the 1930s, Dr. Donald Watt created a revolutionary program called the Experiment in International Living, in which participants immersed themselves in other cultures. Initially, he traveled to Germany and France with twenty-three students, to foster peace through understanding, communication, and cooperation by sharing quarters. This became known as the "home-stay" experience.[3] His idea caught on. Over eighty-five years, more than 70,000 American and international high school students have participated in study abroad and home-stay programs supported by his organization, now called World Learning.

Better known was the visionary Senator J. William Fulbright, who had studied abroad as a youth in the 1920s, pursuing a masters' degree in political science at Oxford University. While there, he experienced the challenge of "culture shock", a time of personal disorientation that often results from having to adapt to a new lifestyle different from one's own. In Fulbright's case, his Arkansas roots severely clashed with the sophisticated atmosphere at Oxford. Fulbright understood early on that a personal international experience was key in pursuing a broader international peace. He felt that the best way to achieve this would be to get out of the classroom, leaving behind abstract notions of culture, so students would have direct, personal interactions overseas. He claimed that in this way we could better understand that other countries are populated not by doctrines that we fear, but by people with the same capacity for pleasure and pain as our neighbors in our own countries.[4] Since it began in 1946, the Fulbright Foundation has become the largest U.S. exchange program. It has offered young American and international adults the support they need to study and conduct research in other countries. Over more than eighty years of operations, Fulbright has sent more than 360,000 participants to 160 countries.

Like Senator Fulbright, President John F. Kennedy was strongly influenced by early overseas travel in Europe. In 1935, he studied at the London School of Economics, but was forced by ill health to return home. He went abroad again in 1937 and spent three months traveling around Europe by car. The next year, he went to work at the U.S Embassy in London while his father was the U.S. Ambassador to the Court of St. James. That is when he wrote his well-known Harvard

University thesis about England's appeasement of Germany, titled *While England Slept*. After completing it, Kennedy went on an extended journey to Latin America, including stops in Colombia, Peru, and Ecuador. He was part of an early breed of 20th century American internationalists.

These travels, together with his daring adventures commanding PT boats in the Pacific during World War II, influenced Kennedy's decision to establish the U.S. Peace Corps in 1961. In describing the new agency's goal, President Kennedy spoke of the U.S. mission to promote world peace and friendship through a Peace Corps, which shall make available to interested countries men and women of the United States who are qualified for service abroad and willing to serve, under conditions of hardship if necessary, to help the peoples of such countries and areas meet their needs for trained manpower.[5]

Generations of young and not-so-young Americans have responded to this call to service. Since the Peace Corps' founding, more than 230,000 Americans have served in 141 countries. Their commitment to work at the grassroots level in developing countries to meet their hosts' needs is seen as the key to building a better, more stable tomorrow. Peace Corps volunteers have demonstrated time and again the very best of American values, including generosity and empathy, and their inimitable, can-do attitudes. Moreover, the Peace Corps has not only shaped the way people in other countries view American democracy, but it has also helped Americans better understand our complex world. This continues to be true today, despite a rising "me-first movement" in the U.S. and leadership efforts to severely curtail funding for international exchange programs.

The spirit of these 20th-century American visionaries has survived to this day but is currently under threat. Many factors are conspiring to reverse the trend towards open borders that characterized the postwar 20th and early 21st centuries. Among these are the dramatic uptick in international refugee and asylum seekers brought on by the continued impoverishment and warfare in a rising numbers of dysfunctional

nation states around the globe. As a result, far-reaching political re-
trenchments now threaten to restrict or even prevent the ease of travel
across borders that many of us in the West have long taken for granted.

We may well be drawing near to a tipping point. We risk losing
our precious right of free movement. This book is meant to serve as a
reminder of how much we all will lose should this happen. So much international goodwill has been promoted, thanks to open borders. Like
earlier American generations, we should draw upon our fortitude to preserve the international peace and stability that our nation has worked
so hard to sustain.

How to Become an American Cultural Ambassador

Step I: Learn How to Co-exist with Other Cultures

It seems my wife Shelly and I have been on a journey of discovery since the day we first met in Tokyo over 30 years ago. Both avid travelers, we'd spent years abroad even before that first day of our study abroad program when we were introduced. Shelly had spent her childhood in Greece and part of her adolescence in Africa. I'd lived in France and Holland. Japan was a logical next step for both of us as we cast our sights towards the still mysterious Orient.

I was smitten by her from the start, but our friendship required special care and attention, as we were busy with our studies and had other romantic relationships. It was only after we had both returned to the United States a year later and were in our home environment that our relationship really started to blossom into a full-fledged romance. From then onward, our shared dream of building an international life across borders really began to take shape.

The world is a diverse and fascinating place, but it's easy to forget that fact when you plod along, submerged in your fixed daily routine.

As we've seen it, the best antidote to that has been to shake up the complacency that often results from living in a single place for too long. Fortunately, our preferred nomadic lifestyle has been entirely do-able for much of our adult lives, since borders have become increasingly porous in many parts of the world. American leadership of the developed world stimulated this era of openness, and Americans have benefited greatly by being mostly welcomed abroad.

Nowadays, when we look back on our accumulated experiences while living in many countries around the world, we've formed strongly held convictions about our country's recent direction. We believe that cross-cultural exchange links forged in the last century by the U.S. government, private sector, and non-profit organizations have promoted a better understanding of one another among the world's family of nations. This, in turn, has created a more peaceful world. Recent political efforts to cut back cultural and educational exchange programs seem sadly short sighted and will inevitably diminish the vast store of accumulated goodwill toward the U.S. that has been the remarkable inheritance left to us by earlier Americans.

In our fast-shrinking world, such programs should be expanding with our full support rather than contracting out of some ill-conceived effort to protect us from imagined foreign threats that are better managed through more contact, not less. All humans on planet Earth are now tightly inter-connected through the inexorable process of globalization—and this won't reverse course in our lifetimes. Even a cursory glance at our increasingly fragile environment, interlinking trade networks, and complex transportation and telecommunications grids reveals how much other cultures influence our daily lives, although often without our conscious awareness. We must learn to cooperate with others or face the potentially calamitous downside of advanced technological terror and cyber-warfare that we as a species will be hard pressed to overcome.

Our travels have led us to a basic acceptance of our common humanity with so many other cultures that co-habit this planet with us. As we've seen it, our foremost task has been to upgrade our knowledge of other cultures and to cultivate a more flexible mindset towards them. We've known for quite some time that individual citizens can no longer enjoy the luxury of leaving cross-cultural relations in the hands of a select few diplomats, generals, or intelligence gatherers. We must all strive to be cultural ambassadors in our daily lives.

We both developed an enduring passion for living overseas while participating in junior year in university programs in Europe in the late 1970s. Shelly participated in a study abroad program at the University of London, while I pursued one at the University of Montpellier in France. My year in France was my first major cross-cultural plunge and it was revelatory in so many ways.

It quickly became clear to me that French students weren't graded on their attendance or participation at either their course lectures or at the smaller seminars that normally accompanied them. In fact, many French instructors graded their students based entirely on their performance on their final oral and written examinations. If certain students chose to work or just laze around during the semester rather than to attend classes regularly, it was quite all right, if they crammed during the final week or two of the term and came up with a passing grade. We American students found this seemingly cavalier attitude created an ever-present temptation to play truant whenever we weren't in the mood to go to class.

Another cultural eye-opener was that most French students lived at home with their families and commuted to classes each day. Dormitories were more the exception than the norm at a French university. Family bonds appeared closer among the French than among our nuclear American families. In the U.S., young adults often move away for college, but in France it was considered unseemly to abandon the warm embrace of family at that stage of life. Indeed, many French adults didn't leave home until marrying, or at least until they'd gotten well established in a career.

Perhaps the most enduring lesson for me from that French culture immersion was that I could view my native country through the prism of a new language and international mindset. I learned how to step back and process a truly alternate reality to the one I'd previously known as a younger person in Middle America. While I'd initially resisted the idea that the daily realities of one culture could be just as valid as those of another, I eventually came to see this as true. It was my first wake-up call to the fact that our individual cultural perceptions are shaped by blinders that limit us from taking in the world's whole glorious, diverse tapestry.

While living in France and steeped in my admittedly cozy academic world, I also came to respect French society a great deal and to admire its awesome historical legacy. Our coursework shined an intense spotlight on such inimitable Gallic political leaders as Charlemagne, Louis XIV, and Napoleon; such superb French artists as David, De La Croix, and the Impressionists; and such brilliant French philosophers as Descartes, Voltaire, and Montesquieu.

———

Several years later, in the mid-1980s, Shelly and I were selected for that fateful semester-long study abroad program in Japan that brought us together. This program was sponsored by the Japanese government and the American Graduate School of International Management (AGSIM), better known as the Thunderbirds. We'd both been nearing the end of our MBA studies in Washington D.C. and were ready for something different to balance the endless lectures and tests we'd endured in graduate school. Separately, we'd been impressed by the economic miracle that Japan had achieved in rebuilding itself from its post-World War II ruins. The two of us were among a small group from the D.C. area that had been selected to participate in this international exchange program in rural Japan.

We became fast friends during the orientation activities in Tokyo, and our friendship continued during several months in residence at our bi-cultural training center on the slopes of Mt. Fuji. Our top-notch orientation to Japan included a tour of Japan's cultural landmarks in Kyoto and Nara and its commercial showcases in Osaka and Nagoya. This trip captivated us from the start, and the fascination we felt seldom waned throughout our time in country.

At our study center near the small town of Fujinomiya, we Americans represented the largest cohort among an international group of about fifty MBA students. There was also a handful of students from Canada, Australia, Korea and France. Our international group was soon living and learning with an even larger group of about two hundred young, promising Japanese executives from a wide swath of Japan's leading enterprises. We lived together in specially designed dormitories that featured single rooms surrounding a large rectangular-shaped common area intended to promote social encounters. The fifteen or so international female participants had their own separate dormitory, since the male-oriented Japanese organizers hadn't selected even one Japanese female executive to participate. That was a strong indicator to us of the deeply embedded chauvinistic attitudes that still prevailed in the Japan of that era.

Our immersion into Japanese culture was further enhanced by shared study projects and regularly scheduled meals with our Japanese colleagues at the campus dining center. The foreign women were integrated as equal participants in all these activities. Thanks to our involvement in this East-meets-West cross-cultural experiment, Shelly and I both acquired the basics of the Japanese language and the start of a respectful understanding of Japanese culture.

At the beginning, though, our foreign cohort was witnessing and reacting strongly to the differing cultural attitudes and behaviors exhibited by our Japanese counterparts. Such things as the high degree of collectivism in Japan, the relative segregation of the sexes in everyday life, and the surprisingly lax attitudes of our Japanese participants towards classroom learning were reshaping certain preconceived ideas we'd had about the country. The cultural portrait of Tokyo that follows this section will delve more deeply into many of the unique dimensions of Japanese society that Shelly and I later experienced during our five years living in Tokyo.

———•———

We learned in those early years that other cultures are complex and worthy of our respect. For the record, I admit that this is our personal account of the several cultures we've explored at length—and it is naturally a highly subjective one. I've used both actual and fictitious names in our story, based whenever possible on the preferences of the individuals involved. Any errors that discerning readers may uncover about cultural practices are the author's and I take full responsibility for them. This tale is intended primarily to open your mind to the many travel and living opportunities that still exist, if you're willing to pursue them. This is our description of the values, patterns of behavior, and cultural heritages we've encountered in our lengthy travel and how they've led to our conscious decision to become American cultural ambassadors in our daily lives.

Step II: Live in Far-flung Places

1: Tokyo, Japan

Taigyo wa shochi ni sumazu.—A Japanese Proverb
(Big Fish Do Not Live in Small Ponds.)

Our first international home together was in a deeply exotic country that in many ways was a mirror-opposite of the United States. We went to live in Tokyo in the late 1980s, a few years after our study-abroad experience in Japan had left us fascinated and wanting more. We were both excited and optimistic about building careers in Tokyo, which was then a booming city in what was arguably the world's most vibrant economy. We had recently married and, of course, we both believed that love would conquer any challenges that such a drastic life change might throw at us.

Rather than arriving in Japan on tourist visas, which would have guaranteed us a maximum of three months there, we came prepared with a written work agreement from my employer, Business International, then part of The Economic Group. This document stated that I'd be submitting several articles a month to Economist-linked publications, for which I'd be paid the going rate for foreign correspondents. This stringer relationship allowed me to apply for a journalist visa with Japanese immigration authorities shortly after arriving in Tokyo. I was fortunate to receive this type of visa, good for one year, and Shelly qualified as my spouse, giving her considerable freedom to work as well.

We were able to successfully renew our visas several times during the five years we lived in Tokyo. This permitted us to work in a variety of fields, including publishing, language teaching, and the non-profit sector. In our final year in Tokyo, we set up our first consulting firm together, serving a wide range of Japanese clients. That was later, though, and before we were able to do that, we had to pay our dues, which meant overcoming difficult personal and cross-cultural adjustments.

Japan was prospering in that era, a time unprecedented in the country's modern history. Thousands of foreigners were flocking there each year to work. Many of us taught English or worked in the English-language sector, which was large and lucrative. Demand for English was seemingly insatiable among the Japanese population in those years. Almost any speaker of English could acquire a local sponsor and a steady job teaching English if he or she was willing to repeat basic English phrases, pore over basic English grammar, correct pronunciation, and smile a lot while practicing small talk with their adult or child students.

Many Japanese took private English lessons even after finishing their formal schooling, owing to their early exposure to the language as youngsters. Their Japanese junior and senior high school English teachers had acquired the language almost entirely by textbook, which meant they often resorted to guessing how to say English words correctly. They ended as masters of English grammar and demanded a grammar-focused curriculum for their students, too. The cycle continued indefinitely, and the few Japanese who seemed to break out of it were the ones who had spent much of their childhoods outside

Japan. Called *kikokushijo*, or returnees, when they came home, these often-fluent English speakers were unfortunately shunned in many cases for outshining their peers and teachers.

For Japanese adults who had lived all or most of their lives in Japan, acquiring some English-language competency was considered almost a patriotic duty, since their country was highly dependent on international trade for its economic success. Japanese brands such as SONY, Panasonic, Toyota, and Mitsubishi were recognized, popular, and associated with high-quality products, but getting them to the world's marketplaces predominantly involved English-language business negotiations, not to mention contracts and marketing campaigns in English.

With many heady successes in those years, some Japanese politicians started to express a national pride bordering on arrogance, considering that Japan had risen like a phoenix from the ashes of World War II. This sentiment was aptly described by Shintaro Ishihara, Japanese politician and former mayor of Tokyo, in his best-selling book *The Japan That Can Say No*.[6] Ishihara proclaimed with a degree of truth that the Japanese business model based on collective decision-making and personal sacrifice for the corporate and national welfare was achieving miraculous results, while Western and more individualistic business approaches were sputtering.

This is hard to imagine today with China's preeminence in Asia, but Japan at the time served as a model for the region's up-and-coming countries. It was also seen as a challenger to U.S. business leadership. American political and business leaders were closely watching Japan for its next strategic moves. This was ironic to us, since Japan had adapted many of its most successful practices from American Edward Deming, including quality control production circles and just-in-time inventories.

———

Since departing Japan at the completion of our exchange program years earlier, returning to Japan had been a goal we'd both agreed upon. We'd planned to set out for Tokyo right after our wedding in Virginia and honeymoon in Mexico. Bidding a sad but excited farewell to family and friends in the Washington D.C. area, we visited with West Coast friends en route to Japan.

Our United Airlines flight from San Francisco to Tokyo took ten hours and by mid-flight our restless cat, who'd been in a cage under our seats, was feeling quite put out. He managed to bolt when one of us opened the door to calm him. He sped down the main cabin aisle to what he no doubt imagined would be a place of refuge under a sleeping woman's legs. As the take-charge newlywed husband, I dutifully headed after him, reaching below the startled woman's legs to grab him by the scruff of the neck just as she awoke. After sincerely apologizing to her, the cat and I moved hurriedly back to our seat at the front of the plane. My duly impressed bride thanked me profusely and we managed to keep his case securely fastened for the duration of the flight.

At Narita Airport, located in the bucolic countryside far from Tokyo, we considered ourselves very lucky when our cat sailed right through the immigration and health inspection processes with only a cursory glance at our documents by the on-duty vet. The Japanese authorities seemed unconcerned about imported cats, so quarantine wasn't an issue for ours. Towards evening that same day, we finally arrived in Tokyo via a shuttle bus and prepared to check in at the business hotel we'd previously reserved. We had chosen such lodgings as the most affordable option, considering how little of our funds remained after the mounting expenses we'd incurred for the wedding, honeymoon, and overseas trip.

Tokyo hotel managers, it turned out, weren't nearly as lax as Japanese immigration officials had been where pets were concerned. There was a strict no-pet policy at our hotel. We had no other option than to keep the poor thing hidden under our several pieces of luggage and assorted overcoats while checking in, all the while hoping he was too exhausted to stir. We were in no better shape ourselves at that point, consumed as we were by jet lag and serious cultural disorientation. Fortunately, the cat slipped by the front desk.

Japanese business hotels offered bare-bones accommodations to their clients, as their ostensible purpose was simply to provide a place to collapse at after a day of marathon meetings. Their rooms featured little more than two twin beds, a Spartan desk, a television set bolted to the wall, a tiny closet for clothes, and a prefabricated bathroom unit. In those days of *endaka*, or the inflated yen, the cost for one night's lodgings was $150 (roughly $300 today) for what were essentially *Motel 6*-style accommodations.

By the next morning, finding cheaper long-term lodgings became our top priority. We headed out early, leaving our kitty behind in the room, as we searched for a place where we could live at least for as long as it would take to secure a long-term apartment in Tokyo. The cash-strapped *gaijin*, or foreigner, looking for a month-to-month living arrangement in those days was mostly stuck with what were euphemistically called *gaijin houses* by the Japanese. These were rather squalid rooming houses that appeared to be reconverted school dormitories located on the fringes of the city, often in undesirable or inconvenient areas. They were occupied by a veritable United Nations of low-budget residents who had come to the Promised Land in search of employment and cash to send back home.

Because of our cat, several of the better-known ones turned us down flat. After a full day of disheartening rejections, we were reaching the bottom of our list of available places. Finally, we happened upon a residence called Fuji House, where we managed to convince the young British manager that our cat would cause no trouble at all. He agreed to rent to us on the condition that the cat would remain in our small six *tatami* mat room and that we would keep him quiet. The room he offered us was virtually the same size as the one in our business hotel, but the cost was significantly less.

———•———

A young African man, the assistant manager at Fuji House, was busy injecting some sort of insecticide into our rice mats as we were led into our designated room. We later learned that *tatami* mats should be changed at least once a year to avoid mite infestations. These mats looked to be maybe a decade old. The room was barren of furniture, with just a few nails on the wall intended for clothing. A quick look behind the sliding doors of our closet revealed two thin, threadbare futon mattresses and two sorry-looking rice pillows awaiting us. We grimly continued with the inspection.

A small window on the wall opposite the door opened onto what looked to be an adjoining machine tool factory, from which we could hear quite clearly the clanging sounds of heavy equipment in constant, repetitive use. This was not exactly the serene Zen-style accommodation many Westerners associate with Japan. Nonetheless, we were in no condition to argue at that moment. We plopped down one week's rent in advance to the young man. Our adjustment to the daily grind of Tokyo was officially beginning.

Like countless other immigrants who were arriving in developed countries around the world, we started at the bottom rung of the social ladder in Japan. What set us apart from other immigrants, though, was our legal status, the fact that we had some income guaranteed to us from the start, thanks to my work contract, and that we had voluntarily chosen to emigrate from our native country. We hadn't been driven out by fear or deprivation. Many of the other residents of Fuji House weren't as fortunate as we were, having fled wars, religious or political persecution, or severe penury at home.

The layout of Fuji House was simple and the facilities primitive. On two crowded floors in one long building, there were fifteen basic rooms with rice-mat floors and sliding, shoji screen closets. There were just two private bathrooms in the building, one for women and one for men, one coin-operated shower, and one over-used washing machine for all forty or so residents. The kitchen consisted of a two-burner stove and an old and oversized refrigerator jammed full of Japanese vegetables, instant noodle packs, and a whole variety of international food staples.

The residents tried to prepare meals that at least somewhat resembled what they might have consumed regularly back home.

Unfortunately, the nearest food providers to Fuji House were of the convenience store variety, so food improvisations were many. African residents, for instance, substituted oatmeal for couscous. We seemed to subsist mostly on instant noodles, sliced cheddar cheese, sugary yo-ghurt, and apples. This was not our normal diet back in the U.S., but it was what we could afford until we earned more income. For our cat, we could find only the cheapest kind of kibble.

Talking to our fellow house residents was our primary source of en-tertainment for a while, since recreational options were limited far out where we lived. Many young men hailed from developing countries of Asia, such as Iran, Bangladesh and the Philippines, and were working long hours as dishwashers, waiters, or day laborers at construction sites. One friendly Iranian man, who had fled his country years earlier, at the time of the 1979 revolution, had worked as a dentist back in Iran. In Tokyo, he'd been working as a waiter at an upscale Italian restaurant and earning enough to support an extended family back home. To the Japanese, his dark Persian looks were indistinguishable from their per-ception of Italian facial features. He was working the lunch and dinner shifts six days a week but managed to produce a big smile whenever we met him.

A young Israeli couple staying just down the hall from us described with dismay their many unsuccessful attempts to secure positions as English-language teachers in Tokyo. Unfortunately, the Japanese equated proper English with the North American and British brands, so even though both Israelis were fluent English speakers and the wife had taught high school English back home, their efforts to teach in Japan proved fruitless. They ended up selling their handmade crafts on the streets of Harajuku, the trendy sector of Tokyo, to make ends meet.

For the month and a half that Shelly and I lived in Fuji House, I couldn't work as a journalist at all. There was no such thing as an Internet connection in those days, and most of my stories had to be typed on the weighty IBM 370/AT desktop computer we had lugged from the U.S. Tom, my work counterpart back in New York, and I had earlier agreed that I'd fax him my story drafts from Tokyo on a weekly basis for him to edit. However, our barren room at Fuji House didn't come equipped with any real workspace, much less a desk. I had to explain to Tom that unforeseeable circumstances had delayed my start-up date as a stringer.

My employer still maintained a representative office in Tokyo's Aoyama neighborhood. However, there had never been a work-sharing arrangement agreed upon by that office and the company's New York headquarters. The Japanese managing director grudgingly allowed me to send the occasional fax to the U.S. It wasn't in the cards for me to do much writing until much later that summer, when we could finally designate a small corner of the apartment we procured as my working space.

We had to learn basic survival skills quickly in our squalid *Gaijin* House. Our stay there in June and early July coincided with the annual rainy season that inundates Japan each year. The rains came fast and furiously and sometimes lingered for days. Having to keep our window closed to ward off raging torrents of water turned our room into a furnace, in which we sweltered both day and night. The best we could do was to purchase a small portable fan to keep the air circulating, but the dampness clung to us like a wet dishrag.

Our poor cat took refuge in a kind of primal stupor closely resembling hibernation, at least during daytime hours. At night he became about as restless as we were, emitting loud and lingering roars periodically, to demand his release. Well, so much for our promise to keep him quiet and unnoticed. There was no real way to contain either him or our feelings of dejection. Every morning, after a seemingly endless night of fitful sleep punctuated by the periodic jolting sounds of passing commuter trains and our unhappy cat, we would crawl out of our humid cave in search of a cup of strong green tea, a few crackers, and anything else we could find.

This lifestyle wasn't exactly what we'd pictured for our new life together just two months into our marriage. We managed somehow to stay sane by remembering the royal treatment we'd received upon arriving in Japan three years earlier as exchange students. That experience had provided us with a great introduction to Japan, Japanese management, the culture, and the language. We'd also enjoyed breaks from classes and traveled to local popular spots, such as the Fuji five lakes region and nearby hot spring resorts. The contrast between that reality and our gloomy present was disorienting, to say the least, but we tried to remind ourselves that Japan had brought us together, so sooner or later things would improve.

———•———

Our luck, or perhaps our hard work, finally paid off. As we were struggling through our second month at Fuji House, we reconnected with a Japanese-American friend from our exchange program. Susy was a can-do person who'd been living in Tokyo and working for a Japanese consulting firm. She was fluent in Japanese and very well connected around town. We shared our sad story with her over a series of beers. She let us ramble on as long as we needed, interrupting only to clarify a few of the details. Finally, she gave us a warm smile and said she might have a solution to our housing crisis. She'd just moved out of her apartment to take up new lodgings in a company-provided one. Her former unit hadn't been rented yet, and she was willing to introduce us to her landlady. Such personal introductions are the way things are supposed to work in Japan. Without them, you might as well go home. We learned that with the right connections, you can meet your basic needs quickly and then start making real progress career-wise.

Susy's place was not much bigger than the *gaijin house* room. It was a ten-*tatami* mat studio, but we'd have our own tiny cooking area and pre-fabricated bathroom. It really had only enough space for one person to live in comfortably by Western standards. Considering where we'd been living, though, we jumped at the chance to have a private apartment centrally located in Takadanobaba, just a few blocks from the central Yamanote train line that circles the city continuously throughout the day and evening.

There were some nice amenities in the six-story *mansion*, or condominium building. One was a staggering view of Tokyo's impressive western sprawl. The owners, Mr. and Mrs. Saito, had designed and built a charming, miniature Japanese garden atop their building. It changed character according to the four seasons: a small cherry tree blossomed in the spring, evergreens flourished throughout the summer, the leaves of miniature deciduous trees changed in autumn, and water froze in a finely crafted fountain in winter. On particularly fine days, from the rooftop we could even see Mount Fuji far off in the distance.

The Saitos showed a surprising openness and good humor toward us in our initial meeting, compared to what we'd expected. Susy made all the necessary introductions and assurances to them as to our sterling personal characters. She explained to them that unlike other *gaijin*, we were used to living in cramped spaces. This was quite true, considering our recent stay in the *gaijin* house and the business hotel.

Our hosts offered us green tea and rice crackers as we settled onto two silk cushions on their rice mats. We did our best to converse intelligibly in our rusty Japanese, with Susy making regular, helpful interjections to convey how much we loved their neighborhood and how greatly we appreciated the trouble they were taking in having foreigners as tenants.

After our small cups had been refreshed a few times, we moved on to a second course of sweet *manju* cakes. Then we finally got down to discussing the terms of the rental contract. We eventually reached an agreement: we could move into the vacant unit early the following week. In exchange, we promised to pay for any damages caused by our cat. By some miracle, they requested just one-half month of *reikin*, or key money. This payment, essentially a tenant bribe to one's landlord, was then a common practice in crowded Tokyo. Normally landlords required a gift equivalent to three month's rent from their new tenants.

The rental housing market in those days was basically a seller's market for landlords, considering how many potential renters were searching for close-in housing to minimize the time spent on Tokyo's packed rail lines. The Saitos also agreed to accept only one month's security deposit, or *shikikin*, which was far less than the three months that was the norm. Overall, we paid a total of one and a half months' rent for these mandatory charges, along with the first month's rent in advance. Had we not had Susy's support, the total up-front fee would likely have been six months' advance rent, plus the first month prepaid for any other Japanese landlord.

After paying out so much, we were left with little money to spare. We reassured ourselves that all would turn out right, as we'd finally turned the corner on our transition to Tokyo. We were starting to hope that life in Japan would be more enjoyable from that point onward. We benefited right away from gestures of goodwill and friendship from the Saitos, and these continued throughout the four years we lived in their cooperative building.

The flexibility of social practices we'd experienced in our negotiations with the Saitos turned out to be characteristic of certain "wet" cultures, which is how Japanese viewed theirs. Collective drinking rituals involving either alcohol or tea in important social situations characterize personal interactions in Japan. Additionally, in a country of lush wet rice fields and cleansing rains from the annual deluge, rules could be bent and one's gut instinct and emotional reactions to people could be relied upon. "Dry" cultures,[7] such as those found in the United States and Western Europe, more closely adhere to a legalistic frame of mind during the many social circumstances and don't bend as much.

A prime lesson we relearned as two individualistic Americans was to ask friends and acquaintances for help during difficult transitions. Susy had solved our immediate problem and had created bridges for us to make critical new acquaintances, while also working out a very good deal for her two unseasoned charges. Because both Shelly and I had been trained in the hard-nosed game of self-promotion in B-School, we learned this different approach called for a degree of humility that had previously been unfamiliar to us. However, the longer we stayed in Tokyo, the more it became second nature to us.

———

Fast on the heels of moving into our new apartment, I tried to jumpstart my work as a stringer for *The Economist*. I cleared away a corner of our tiny apartment and set up a very crowded workspace with my desktop computer, files with contact lists and story ideas, and a tray of office supplies. Unfortunately, this clutter was hardly a conducive arrangement for serious journalism. I experimented with working at different times of day and evening that wouldn't interfere with our domestic schedule, but there was never any door to close behind me. There also seemed to be no way of avoiding our now revived kitty and our curious and visible neighbors. Our home landline was also doing double duty as my work point of contact, which caused a few headaches.

Back in New York, my colleague Tom, who was serving as my liaison to senior management, had a knack for calling us when we were sound asleep in Tokyo. New York is fourteen hours behind Tokyo for much of the year, so the start of the workday there coincides with sleepy time in Tokyo. While Tom was raring to go in the mid-morning of his time, we were jolted out of a sound sleep when his calls came through. What invariably resulted for me was a feeling of disjointedness that Tom never understood. He claimed never to experience jetlag when he traveled. I wasn't sure if that was possible or if he was deluding himself.

Our communication misunderstandings were compounded by the less-than-clear landline reception that plagued transoceanic calls in those days. As we each tried to follow the conversational thread, we would be talking over the other's phone echo, resulting in time wasted and nerves frazzled. Eventually I began to rely on the fax machine rather than the phone for communicating important news to him. I could then conveniently leave the phone off the hook at night to ensure our peaceful slumber.

During our first three months at our new residence in Takadanobaba, the list of stories I wrote and sent back to New York was a short one.

The conditions just weren't right for my work in a cramped home. We soon realized that our professional lives had to move in a new direction, and that would involve finding gainful employment in non-freelance areas.

On the bright side, we had finally gotten stable housing and a long-term visa for working legally in Japan. The limits of what we could do were constrained only by our relative ignorance of actual working conditions in Tokyo and our limited ability to communicate in spoken Japanese. Both of us were stuck at the advanced beginner level, having studied the language for just one semester as graduate students three years earlier. We were lucky that economic conditions were still so good in Japan that two hard-working *gaijin* could land well-paid employment without having a complete toolkit of professional skills.

In retrospect, it's clear we both could have reached out to our friends and acquaintances to gain full-time employment at this point. At that time, though, our Tokyo-based network of professional contacts consisted mostly of former Japanese school colleagues who all seemed to be working inhuman hours at traditional Japanese corporations and banks. Shelly and I were both hoping for something different, more creative, and preferably with bearable working conditions.

We sought job opportunities each day in the English-language newspaper, *The Japan Times,* which featured a host of employment advertisements. We scanned the paper the old-fashioned way, identifying full-time jobs and circling them with a highlighter pen. We pinpointed those within the English-language publishing and teaching areas, the international sector, or at non-profit organizations. Japan possessed an incredibly large market for English language teaching and learning materials, with English language skills widely perceived as an absolute must to support the country's enormous corporate export machine. English language brochures, corporate reports, and all kinds of promotional materials were needed in great abundance to educate the world about Japan's latest product miracles and corporate success stories.

The two of us nailed salaried positions in no time. Shelly's new employer was a non-profit organization specializing in sending Japanese students to American home-stay families and, less frequently, bringing American students to Japan. Located in Tokyo, it was a small office of seven or eight employees who seemed like family. Shelly served as the firm's resident expert on American exchange programs, having managed such cross-cultural activities previously in Virginia before we were married. The job was a good fit for her from the start, although the scope of her work was limited, except for a few periods of frantic activity during a typical academic exchange year.

I replied to a notice for an English-language copywriter and editor, forwarding my resume and cover letter to the organization. I followed up with a phone call a few days later. As Japan was exporting to a world marketplace and starting to ramp up its already sizeable overseas foreign direct investment, there was a steady demand in Tokyo for technical writers of English who possessed a basic knowledge of Japanese business. My prior studies in Japan and earlier work with business publishing in New York ensured that I met their basic requirements. At the interview, I received an offer right away—and at a salary that seemed princely compared to my meager earnings as a stringer. We could finally catch our breath, knowing that a steady flow of yen would soon be coming our way.

———•———

I'll use the pseudonym Information Kaisha, or IK, to describe my Japanese employer, who was a major player in the field of English-language investor relations and publicity back then. IK relied on a management approach that was quite un-Japanese, although I wasn't aware of it at the time I accepted the job. It soon became obvious, though, that the roughly thirty employees in the firm deferred to the *shacho*, or president, who had founded the firm and was its driving force.

Because of *Shacho's* tendency to show anger in stressful situations – another un-Japanese attribute – he employed an *amakudarai*, or retired Japanese executive, to defuse and deflect tense situations. This elderly gentleman possessed the requisite polish and English-language skills to serve as the main point of contact for hiring and managing the firm's five or six foreign employees. Even this senior staff member, a man everyone called *Bucho*, or division manager, was ultimately held hostage to the *shacho's* whims.

Ironically, the big boss could only speak a little English and often struggled to communicate effectively with his foreign staff. *Shacho* never felt very comfortable with English, but the reality of the Japanese marketplace made it inevitable that our most profitable publications would be produced in English. Our principal clients understood that they'd have to pay a premium to procure the talents of Tokyo-based foreign professionals.

Our desks at IK were organized in three long rows that faced you as you entered our Ginza-area office. In the foreground, to the right, sat the dedicated core of young Japanese sales representatives, mostly male, who scoured the city daily in search of fresh account prospects, nabbing them when they could, and working together with them on a portfolio of printed products to be produced by IK. These sales reps managed things all the way from the account signing ceremony to the delivery of our completed end-products weeks or even months later.

Scanning the office further, your gaze would then have settled upon the creative people, including several Japanese designers, in the center row of desks. Finally, looking across to the far side of the room, you'd have seen the Western copywriters and editors in the row directly adjacent to a long bank of windows that were nearly always thrown open, regardless of the season. It was never clear to me why the foreign employees were allotted what seemed to be the most coveted locations in the office.

Our foreign cohort was a motley mix of five men and one woman, including three Americans, an Australian woman, a New Zealander, and a Brit. We were given the task of finding a consistent English-language voice for our company's diverse array of annual reports, executive speeches, and company newsletters that we churned out regularly. To be candid, most of our Japanese readers would probably not have been able to spot a difference in tone or English-language consistency.

Nevertheless, we did our best to achieve this common voice that tended towards Midwestern American English, perhaps owing to the near majority of the three Americans.

Shacho and his able sales representatives, to their credit, succeeded in opening the spigot to a steady stream of jobs that kept us humming at our keyboards most work days. Our client base was pulled from a veritable *Who's Who?* of successful Japanese companies, including Panasonic, Mitsubishi, Nissan, and Toshiba. As busy as we were in keeping up with the daily workload, I tried to observe our office with a critical eye and reflect on how it operated in contrast to my earlier workplaces in the U.S. The differences were numerous and illuminating.

What follows are my best efforts to capture the prevailing Japanese workplace mindset and rules at the time. The lessons I learned and their implications for those who worked with Japanese partners were the following:

A good attendance record and attitude outweighed one's actual achievements.

The ability to fit in was highly respected by the Japanese. An individual who overly promoted his abilities and achievements ended up not being appreciated by work colleagues. There is a Japanese expression for this point: *deru kugi wa utareru*, or "the protruding nail will be hammered down". This feature of a Japanese office was the source of painful learning for most of us Westerners. Our eyes always seemed to be focused on productivity and quality improvements. This hardly mattered to our Japanese supervisors.

Sooner or later, one of us would blurt out something about someone's slapdash efforts or about some ridiculous language errors that had slipped through the production process. Normally, the management's response would be a polite thank you for our comments, followed by little or no action to reprimand the guilty party. We foreigners learned to tone down our outspokenness on such matters.

Complaints needed to be held in check.

The Japanese capacity for enduring situations that might have seemed intolerable to those of us from other cultures was frequently apparent in our work environment. The Japanese tended to *gaman suru* ("grit things out"), rather than voice a complaint or refuse an unreasonable order. This spirit of self-sacrifice prevailed at IK. It was particularly evident whenever a looming deadline required an unambiguous management request for us to work overtime to get a critical job completed in a limited time. While the Western bloc in the office would start mobilizing in opposition to the requested late night or weekend work, the long-suffering Japanese contingent would, as a rule, hold their tongues.

From the Japanese perspective, there was no other plausible way to meet a strict deadline than to work harder—never mind asking why the deadlines hadn't been negotiated differently in the first place. They would merely shrug their shoulders with resignation while muttering the eponymous phrase *sho ga nai* ("it can't be helped").

When in doubt, it was best to defer to authority.

The rank-and-file Japanese employees, at least in those days, tried to keep their heads down with their inner eyes targeted firmly on the prize. Given time, training, and the proper seasoning, the male employees at least would eventually rise to positions of authority. In the local dialect, this approach was described as *ishi no ue ni mo sannen kan*, "perseverance overcomes all things".

This deeply ingrained notion in the Japanese psyche was to take your time in performing anything worth doing. Eventually you'd acquire a mastery of it and, assuming you maintained the right mental discipline, you'd benefit in the long term. In the short term, though, it was wise to look to more senior figures for guidance on the most pressing company issues.

In meetings or negotiation sessions with clients, the most senior officials were the ones who'd sit directly opposite one another at the center of the table. Either they or their appointed spokesmen would conduct most of the substantive discussions. Lower-ranking employees, me included, would limit their comments to a few desultory remarks during the preliminary small talk phase or would speak only in direct reply to a request for specific information related to their jobs. I learned to accept this supporting role graciously within the Japanese work context. In truth, I found it much more exhausting to sit silently through a long, drawn-out meeting than to participate actively.

Spread the risk and thus the blame.

Japanese employees tried to forge a consensus in making important decisions, ostensibly to promote group harmony. In fact, most of the time this resembled more of an attempt to pass along some piece of information from one person to another. Eventually, any bad news of a wrong decision or an ineffective work practice would dissolve and with it any blame for those involved. This was the opposite of the blame game we play in the West, whereby a story gets worse and worse the more it is shared, with the scapegoat getting even guiltier as the rumor mill continues to churn.

At IK, gatekeepers, including the *bucho*, served as disseminators and managers of negative information. Their job was to translate the negative into something palatable for the foreign staff's public consumption. *Shacho*, for instance, was often the bearer of bad news. For example, he might issue a terse rejection to a joint plea by the foreign staff for newer office equipment or additional time off. *Bucho*, acting as our cultural interpreter, would cleverly rephrase *Shacho's* edict as a pensive phrase such as *tabun itsuka*, or roughly, "We'll consider that sometime later".

The main cultural lesson to be drawn from this was that modes of behavior in Japanese and Western workplaces differed markedly. While personal interaction in a Japanese office could often be formal and ritualized to the extreme, outside of the office, behaviors could be surprisingly spontaneous and dynamic, especially when alcohol was involved. The following incident is a case in point.

During my second year working at IK, I participated in an elaborate dinner held on behalf of an important client, the Japan National Railways, held at a formal Japanese inn in Tokyo. This event was organized by *Shacho* with the purpose of reestablishing a teetering relationship with this esteemed client. It all comes back to me in a murky rush of fascination and shame.

As the evening began, we were all seated at a long table. Our side included *Shacho*, his trusty Japanese artistic director, the chief writer (me) and the head of proofreading, an unflappable Australian woman. On the other side of the table sat four hard working and stoic middle managers from our client organization, a major Japanese railroad company. Five kimono-clad hostesses, including three veteran *geishas* and two apprentices, did the serving and entertaining. When not hurrying to collect our plates for six courses of exquisite food, each hostess knelt between two guests. Three positioned themselves on our side of the table and two on the other. All of us were coddled and catered to by our overly solicitous servers, who continuously filled our sake cups and beer mugs, all the while maintaining a surprisingly raunchy patter of lewd tales and obsequious questions.

Considering that I only understood about half of what they were saying in their playful but obscure dialect, I tried to play along. Cigarettes were lit and relit by our hostesses, so a viscous cloud of smoke eventually settled over our table and never quite dissipated. The intent was clear soon enough, to see which ones of us would embarrass ourselves the most in a fit of high-spirited drunkenness. Our bemused female colleague struggled to maintain her pretense of insouciance amid all the adolescent male antics fast unfolding.

As the resident cultural explorer, I tried to focus on the facial expressions and postures of our hostesses, my colleagues, and our sourpuss clients. The veteran *geisha* appeared to me as thoroughly rehearsed actresses, as if they had staged this performance a thousand times previously. Their laughter appeared forced and drawn out in the ritualized manner of *kabuki* performers. The younger ones moved rather reluctantly, as if they were being coerced into the staged merriment and never seemed quite confident that they could rise to the occasion.

Shacho and the art director were doing their utmost to keep the mood lively. At one point, *Shacho* reached over and pinched one of the younger hostesses on her hind-quarter, which triggered a long plaintive wail of mock protest. Just as we were absorbing this, the art director drunkenly tipped over a large bottle of beer right into the *shacho's* lap, triggering pandemonium. Suddenly, the entire flock of *geishas* and hostesses was surging toward him with hot and dry towels in hand and *kimonos* of all colors flying. They were ministering to his lap and other drenched areas on his body. He seemed both flustered and enthralled by the intensity of their ministrations.

Our clients, for their part, failed to crack a smile even at the peak of the excitement. Nonetheless, our unflappable leader still managed to recover. He continued smiling as we bade our collective farewells a short time later. He even paused to plant a sloppy, intoxicated kiss on the cheek of an elderly *geisha*. The rest of us staggered out behind him into the early Tokyo morning, in search of taxis to deliver us home.

The next morning at the office, the entire incident seemed to have been forgotten and none of the Japanese participants referred to it ever again, at least publicly. My efforts to inquire further about it were basically rebuffed with a shrug and a small nervous laugh on their parts. It seemed to be an unwritten law of my Japanese workplace that embarrassing incidents committed while drunk weren't later acknowledged or even discussed. Of course, I wasn't very well schooled in matters that appeared to be known implicitly by my local colleagues.

This built-in understanding of appropriate behavior shared by a specific group of people is referred to in the field of culture studies as being part of their "small c" culture[8]. This term refers to the many hidden aspects of a culture, such as shared values, mindsets, and behaviors that are often invisible or indecipherable to the casual visitor. A distinction is regularly made between this type of culture and "Big C" Culture, which is more obvious to all and generally includes literature, cooking, music, art, and artifacts. This latter definition is what most people have traditionally understood as representing the cultures of distinct ethnic or social groups.

While we were at work, mystifying daily incidents involving "small c" culture convinced Shelly and me that we needed a more profound understanding of the vast cultural gap that existed between the Japanese and us. We were badly in need of cultural coping strategies. We inquired of friends and searched in the local English language press, including the *Tokyo Journal*, for any information we could find about cultural and educational programs for foreign residents in Tokyo.

We soon learned about a fledgling intercultural group called *Ibunkakan Kommunikeshion Kenkyukai*, better known as the Society for Intercultural Education, Research and Training (SIETAR). Initially composed of just a few Tokyo-based professionals working in the growing field of Intercultural Communication (IC), the group was expanding at that time into a larger umbrella organization that included university professors, researchers, company trainers, international corporate staffers, and English teachers.

SIETAR's mission was to educate Japanese going abroad and foreigners coming to Japan, to better understand cultural differences and effectively adapt for a better intercultural experience. The group also aspired to educate the Japanese public about differing values, behaviors, and assumptions that prevailed between the Japanese and other populations. Over the next few years, we feasted on a full menu of meetings and workshops focusing on communication style differences, diverse adult learning approaches, theories of culture, and the varying attitudes of East and West.

At SIETAR events, we regularly met inspiring colleagues, many of whom became friends. One friend, Shoko Araki, had established her own intercultural training and support group in Tokyo called *Cross Cultural Training Services* (CCTS). She was offering two—and three-day intercultural workshops featuring leading figures in the IC field from the United States.

Shelly and I participated in several of her workshops led by Dr. Janet Bennett and Dr. Milton Bennett, who were the co-directors of the Intercultural Institute in Portland, Oregon, as well as Dr. Dean Barnlund, professor of Intercultural Communication at San Francisco State University, and Dr. Sheila Ramsey, who specialized in intercultural sensitivity training. They all coached us in how to perceive things from an intercultural perspective. We are greatly indebted to them.

This process required certain personal attributes and a proactive mental attitude. According to Ramsey, intercultural interaction is an art form that requires flexible intelligence, integrated awareness, a concern for others, and a willingness to trust one's instincts.[9] In our daily lives from then onwards, we tried to look inwardly whenever possible before attempting to explain puzzling or disturbing cross-cultural encounters.

One particularly good IC model the Bennetts shared was called Describe-Interpret-Evaluate, or D-I-E. While the acronym may seem ominous, the model can provide keener insights and better decision-making skills when immersed in other cultural contexts. The model works as follows: When you observe an incident in a foreign culture that seems strange or different, it's best to first describe it in detail to colleagues or friends. Without jumping to any immediate conclusions, you should include as many related details as possible concerning what you have seen.

Your description should paint a picture of the persons involved, the setting of the incident, the timing, and the chronology of events. When you have shared all that you can recall, the next step should be to interpret what may have transpired in as many ways as you can without forming any immediate value judgments. These possible interpretations should be shared with a person from the other culture to elicit the best explanation for what took place. Your final step—evaluating the incident—should take place within this more informed context created by the describe-and- interpret phases.

In applying the D-I-E model, I revisited the geisha party incident and the curious silence by my Japanese co-workers the morning after. In utilizing this cultural model, I described what had happened several times to Shelly and SIETAR members. A group discussion of the incident by Japanese and Western group members led to several possible cultural interpretations. One was that my work colleagues truly couldn't remember what had happened the previous evening, owing to the huge amount of liquor they'd consumed. Most of the group didn't find this to be the best interpretation, considering that these same colleagues went out drinking nearly every night and didn't clam up in the same manner after other outings.

Another interpretation was that the event had been so embarrassing for all concerned that they couldn't even bear to discuss it in the light of day. While that seemed plausible at first, upon later reflection, it seemed less likely because most of my coworkers had been with the company for several years and had probably seen similar behaviors on other occasions. Yet another interpretation of why they'd remained silent was that the uproarious antics were simply viewed as normal behavior in that type of social situation and didn't merit any further discussion. That didn't seem quite right, though, considering that it was quite rare for our foreign staff members to be invited to such a late-night event with the *shacho*. There had been nothing at all normal about that night out.

Having discussed this in great depth with the resident cultural experts, one evaluation of the incident made the most sense from a cross-cultural perspective. The evening had been a huge failure for our firm in its efforts to repair a damaged relationship with an important client. This meant our firm had lost face, suffered a public shaming. This was particularly bad for the *shacho*. Public acknowledgment of such a negative outcome wasn't permissible within our workplace context. Our staff members were mortified and too scared to talk about what had transpired, lest *Shacho* hear them gossiping and think negatively about them.

Our intercultural trainers, whom Shelly and I came to recognize as invaluable gurus, provided us with many other compelling theories for digesting and processing cultural incidents of this type. These theories greatly enhanced our understanding of cross-cultural differences between East and West, while also raising our effectiveness on our jobs. Our trainers served as our earliest role models for what it meant to be both inter-culturally capable and globally-minded citizens. We've tried to follow their examples in the ensuing years.

Thanks to the support of SIETAR and CCTS, we began to feel increasingly confident about understanding our Japanese hosts in daily life. That still left us with the task of upgrading our language skills to better perform at work and develop smoother relationships with friends and neighbors. For this, we didn't have to look far. Located just one train stop away from us on the Yamanote line was a volunteer service group specifically focused on providing Japanese language and culture lessons to foreigners living in Tokyo. Called *Chihaya Nihongo Kenshukai*, it was staffed by a small group of trained and dedicated Japanese language instructors.

In an article I was writing for a local English language newspaper, the founder of the group, Yayoi, explained that her inspiration for forming the group had been an account she'd read of a young South Asian student who'd starved to death in Tokyo. Shocked that such a thing could have occurred in Japan, she became increasingly sensitized to the plight of foreign residents in the country. To her surprise, many foreign students suffered from social isolation and were struggling with basic survival, due to limited funds and language capabilities. She solicited the help of other concerned citizens, including lawyers, executives, and teachers, in organizing her non-profit group.

The teaching method instructors at Chihaya employed was called the Scientific Direct Method (SDM,) which emphasized situational dialogues and basic sentence patterns encountered in daily life.[10] In contrast to more traditional teaching approaches, the SDM encouraged the instructor to incorporate slang and popular idioms into their lessons to achieve realistic spoken communication. During our first two years in

Tokyo, we managed to progress from advanced basic level to intermediate level Japanese under the friendly tutelage of our Chihaya instructors.

Overall, the focus of their classes was to help their students achieve oral competence. For those with a special interest in writing, they also offered texts that included a step-by-step introduction to the brush strokes required for writing *kana*, Japan's native alphabet widely used for basic words and ideas, as well as *kanji*, the Chinese alphabet that is used for more complex thoughts and phrases. While Shelly and I mastered the twenty-six-character *kana* alphabet (referred to as *hiragana*), neither of us was ever able to progress past recognizing one hundred or so Chinese characters. Fortunately, Japan eases the language burden for foreign visitors by also employing a Romanized alphabet, called *romaji*, for a large percentage of public signs, billboards, railway notices, and other public service announcements.

With our professional and language support groups as cultural mentors, we began to gain our footing in Tokyo and at work more specifically. But even as our knowledge and skills continued to grow, our daily challenges persisted. For instance, as a taller-than-average Westerner, I was forever running into low-hanging ledges and feeling hemmed in by our tiny, ten-rice mat apartment. At work, our work space was especially limited from a Western perspective. As Edward T. Hall, the noted anthropologist, observed in his landmark study of spatial perceptions, every culture develops its own concept of appropriate personal distance. Hall found that American workers who could push away from their desks to achieve a certain amount of distance would identify their work space as adequate.[11]

My personal space at IK wasn't anywhere near adequate by that definition. In my tiny cubicle, besides my modest desk and chair, I managed to cram in a few essentials: a desktop computer, a bookshelf, a small file cabinet, and a lamp. When engaged in a phone conversation, I had no way of avoiding the ongoing chatter of my colleagues, although my ability to concentrate on my high-priority projects improved over time. Eventually I resorted to wearing headphones while working; they allowed me to focus, but I risked creating an anti-social image for myself in the eyes of my coworkers. The phone system didn't help. When incoming calls were received by a centralized switchboard service, the operator called out the name of the person requested on a public intercom system. At times I didn't hear my name called and a co-worker would have to tap me on the shoulder.

The office layout simply didn't permit a comfort zone for the foreign employees. Of our thirty or so employees, all but the two senior managers occupied the large bull pen space that constituted our main office. The two individual offices on the back perimeter were reserved for the *shacho* and his loyal lieutenant, the elderly *bucho*. Hall believed that many Japanese preferred being packed in together at work. My Japanese co-workers appeared to take the crowding in stride.

The two aisles between our three rows of desks afforded just enough space for two average-sized Japanese employees to squeeze by one another. Whenever one foreign and one Japanese employee, or two foreign employees encountered each other in the aisle, one or the other had to backpedal to allow for passage to the other. For me, this lack of a manageable egress, combined with the proximity of desks aligned one right next to another, caused a sense of claustrophobia.

Added to this was the fact that smoking was permitted in our workplace and the situation became almost unbearable. I kept a small oscillating fan perched on the edge of my desk and turned it outwards in the hope of dispersing the smoke. This only partly succeeded. We non-smokers ingested huge amounts of second-hand smoke. I wonder to this day whether my susceptibility to chest congestion is directly related to my time spent at IK. This crowded, loud, and smoky setting led to illnesses, especially of the respiratory sort. Loud hacking and chronic coughs were heard throughout the year, but especially in winter when the windows were kept closed most of the time.

The range of permissible behaviors tended to be looser for foreign employees than for Japanese employees. My straying from prescribed office etiquette at times was chalked up to *gaijin,* "eccentricity". We outsiders were grudgingly permitted to take more sick leave than our Japanese peers. We also took longer vacations and longer lunch hours and went home earlier at the end of most workdays. We often employed an opt- out excuse for what we believed were overly restrictive cultural norms in Japan, compared to what existed back in our home countries. We would explain to our local hosts that we just couldn't adapt to such rigorous behavioral standards and would basically refuse to adhere to them.

Tokyo is rightly celebrated for its world-class restaurants. In recent years, it has boasted more Michelin-rated restaurants than any other city in the world. However, most of these high-end restaurants were far beyond my pay grade at the time, except for the very occasional splurge on a special occasion. Ironically, the splurge occurred outside Tokyo.

That memorable occasion was a visit Shelly and I made to Kyoto, to admire the city's fall foliage. We began a sparkling fall day there with a long and lingering visit to Kiyomizu temple, known for its gorgeous wood-crafted pavilions and unmatched natural setting. After touring the temple grounds and taking a refreshing break to sip green tea and snack on Japanese rice crackers, we proceeded to our lunch at a traditional *ryokan,* or inn, in the Gion section of town.

This was our first and only experience of *kaiseki-ryori,* Japan's remarkable food ceremony, in which each guest is presented with one bejeweled artistically presented dish after another. The food is meant to approximate the stunningly beautiful colors of nature that were on display just outside our window as we lunched. *Kaiseki-ryori* changes colors and flavors with the seasons, striving to mesh as much as possible with the natural environment. On that November afternoon, we sat on cushions situated on the traditional *tatami* mat floors, savoring every morsel of our *shiso* leaves, followed by burdock roots, and then gingko fruit, and so on. It was a sublime experience. Our lunch stretched out for hours—we've never enjoyed a meal more. Of course, such a culinary treat was not to be had without an eye-popping price tag. The bill for two amounted to 30,000 yen, or roughly $250 in those days.

Back in Tokyo, eating was usually a much more pedestrian experience for us. Virtually the entire working population of Tokyo went to lunch from noon to one o'clock. The result was often a mass of hungry, hurried humanity wanting to eat. Lunchgoers congregated in single-sex groups. *Salarimen*, white-collar male workers, normally headed to the company cafeteria, a nearby soba shop, or to any convenient Japanese restaurant for a no-nonsense economical meal.

Office ladies, the female support staff members who carried the load in nearly every company, tended to go in groups to Western-style coffee shops or department store restaurants, more for their trendy ambience than for their food. Besieged restaurant owners had little alternative but to offer a few prescribed luncheons: consisting of a soup or salad, spaghetti or a sandwich plate, and coffee or tea.

At the Japanese restaurants, a variant might be miso soup, followed by pork or tempura cutlet on rice, and green or oolong tea to wash it down. The Japanese set tended to be the better choice of the two. The miso soup, an earthy brown soup laced with chunks of tofu and bits of scallion, never failed to warm and satisfy me. Likewise, most Japanese rice dishes proved to be hearty, nutritious, and appetizing. I've never tasted a bad green tea. The Western fare, on the other hand, was often bland. For lunch, the Japanese idea of Western-style soup turned out to be an insipid consommé that was followed by a gummy, watery mound of spaghetti with just a hint of tomato sauce. This was finished off with an inky cup of coffee.

Those who preferred a restaurant sandwich were served two thin slices of pale white bread with the crusts carefully removed for optimal visual effect. The micro-thin spread of mayonnaise, egg, and cucumber would barely quench one's hunger pangs after a hard morning's work. In truth, Western sets worked better as light snacks than as true meals.

At the peak of Japan's economic boom in the 1980s and early 1990s, one phenomenon that received a lot of attention in the Japanese media was the tragic problem of *karoshii*, working oneself to death. It occurred with surprising frequency in a country where work dominated everyone's waking hours to an extent unheard of in other industrialized countries. Tokyo won hands down when compared to Western cities in terms of total working hours per week, company expectations of employee loyalty, and the significance that work had in defining one's status and shaping one's lifestyle and friends.

The Japanese tolerated their workaholic lifestyle as a kind of badge of honor. The insidious marriage of company and personal life could be seen on so many occasions. The boss was often a *nakodo*, matchmaker, who would introduce two young people hoping to marry. For that reason, bosses were often accorded places of honor at wedding ceremonies and were encouraged to make the most important toasts to the good health of the couple. After the wedding, brides were frequently urged to retire from their jobs and turn their attention to the important tasks of homemaking and child rearing.

The company's influence on the individual was also evident in the widespread use of *meishi*, name cards, both at work and in purely social occasions. Upon meeting someone for the first time, the single most important act was the exchange of *meishi*. Without this ritualized gesture, social interactions would become stilted. Name cards provided a way to interact appropriately and allowed for the playing out of well-rehearsed scripts, which involved comments on one's company and position and inquiries about possible friends they might have in common. Without the cards, the players would have had to ad lib their roles, a predicament most Japanese preferred to avoid. While name cards are also used to varying extents in Western cultures, it is the rare Westerner who carries stacks of name cards to the golf course, a wedding, or a vacation resort.

Work and identity have long been tightly bound in Japan. For much of the post-World War II era and up until the early 1990s, Tokyo's amazingly productive and self-sacrificing office workers labored ceaselessly to reconstruct a city that had been strafed and left in ruins by the final months of the war. Not surprisingly, most Japanese viewed life and work as fundamentally one and the same. Only at the end of the boom years did a substantial number of people start to wonder if perhaps life meant more than climbing the corporate ranks.

The economic stagnation that eventually took root provided an opening for a Western-style interpretation of the separation of work and private lives. Some people began asserting that the individual had the right to expect certain freedoms from group responsibilities, and even to pursue their own interests. However, they were attempting to unclench the collectivist grip on an exceedingly clannish and traditional society. Social change was not going to come easily.

Fighting an uphill battle, certain new leaders in Japan still felt that increasing the amount of leisure time would serve the national interest. Japan Broadcasting Company (NHK), for instance, ran a well-received series in 1990 entitled "Why are you married to your company?" It sought opinions from everyday Japanese workers and from foreigners, including me, about the national obsession with work. I remember the interviewer asking me how perceptions of work in Japan compared with those in the United States. I emphasized the clear line of demarcation we draw in the U.S. between our work lives from Monday to Friday and our private lives the rest of the time. Ironically, the interview was conducted at IK's office at eight o'clock at night on a weekday. I was still there, of course.

The Japanese Ministry of Transport also sent out a team of "leisure specialists" to study the non-work time activities in other countries, including Australia and the West Coast of the United States, where the art of taking it easy was deeply rooted. The study detailed many facets of leisure and offered an action plan to promote greater relaxation in Japan. One recommendation was the official closing of government offices and banks on weekends. Previously office workers for those large institutions had been working at least a half-day on Saturdays. Despite this initiative, many of the workers still felt duty-bound to prove their undying company loyalty. They either stayed longer on weeknights or came in anyway on Saturdays.

For those who followed the new directive, many felt immobilized by the stretches of free time that required no planning and offered no supervision. One option was to while away their time in *pachinko*, Japanese-style pinball parlors, which required a minimal attention span to focus on the silver balls falling incessantly into tiny slots built into the game board. Drinking also became an even more popular activity than it already had been. This was not surprising, considering how many drinking establishments there were in Tokyo. For many, it was far easier to head to the local tavern than to arrange a tennis match or golf outing with friends. In the case of tennis, court times and dates normally had to be booked far ahead of time. For golf, long drives in heavy traffic to bucolic country courses were required. Golf fees were exorbitant, leading to a widespread public perception of the game as elitist.

A sizeable number of Tokyoites, including most foreigners, spent many an evening carousing in local *izakayas*, bars, to the point of inebriation. Foreign residents felt motivated to reduce the stress associated with their status as a perpetual outsider among the mostly homogenous Japanese population. We *gaijin* stood out in the crowd. On many occasions, Shelly and I were surrounded by pointing, giggling, screaming Japanese schoolchildren on visits outside Tokyo, where the sight of foreigners was still a novelty. There were certain times when we wanted to crawl under a rock and disappear.

My occasional drinking binges during my student days in Japan had offered an opportunity to let off steam and meet new friends. It didn't seem to matter too much that I would awaken the next morning feeling like a soiled dishrag. This changed after I joined a Japanese company. I started to associate drinking with my work obligations and the act consequently became less pleasurable. I didn't see it as a leisure time activity. Rather, I understood it for what it was: an essential way of maintaining cordial relations with colleagues and clients.

For stress reduction, a better option for me was working out at the local sports center in Shinjuku ward. Later, I joined an upscale private health club on Omote Sando Boulevard. Fortunately, Tokyo's twenty-three municipal wards offered low-cost public exercise facilities that were open daily. For a minimal fee, it was possible to enjoy swimming, weight training, table tennis, kendo, archery and other pursuits. These places were the favored haunts of mothers with children in the mornings and boisterous adolescents in the afternoons. In the peak after-school hours, you had to be a contortionist to claim a spot in the locker room. It was possible to complete a workout provided you didn't mind fifteen-minute waits at the life cycles, training equipment, or to dive into a lane in the packed swimming pool. If you arrived after seven o'clock at night, the facilities were more manageable and populated mostly by adults.

After we'd reached our saturation point with these, we pleaded with Susy to introduce us to her more civilized private club in Tokyo's fashionable Harajuku district. Upon entering the rooftop club, which was called XAX, we were immediately dazzled by the shiny, state-of-the-art training machines, polished wood floor dance studio, and charming miniature swimming pool with an adjacent sun deck. A chorus of *konnichi wa's* (hellos) from healthy-looking young ladies at the reception desk greeted us. Before our first solo workout, we were required to undergo a rather exhaustive screening process that included a written questionnaire about our overall state of health and any previous sports injuries we had incurred.

After completing this, we followed it up with a one-hour healthy lifestyle chat and club introduction by the certified American trainer in residence. During our lifestyle examination, the expert advised me that my systolic blood pressure was a bit high—not surprising, considering my frenetic lifestyle at the time—but that my body fat level was a low, low twelve percent. He measured this with the aid of a device resembling a cattle prod that he attached to my mid-section, where love handles appeared years later. Knowing how trim, or rather how underfed, I already was, we started constructing a strategy that would beef up my shoulders and biceps with a corresponding cardio improvement plan that would lower my blood pressure.

During each successive visit to our new home-away-from home, Shelly and I would carefully map our progress on our customized health profile form and would record the number of repetitions for our weight-training machines and the number of minutes we spent on the treadmill, in the pool, or on the lifecycles. Shelly also joined aerobic dance classes at the club. By the end of three months, I was pleased with my ten percent decrease in blood pressure, my increase in weight by two kilograms, and a noticeable improvement in my mental outlook and overall health. Shelly's results were similarly positive, although her aim had been more focused on achieving finely-toned muscle rather than useless flab, as described by our trainer. We were feeling magically removed from the daily grind of the Tokyo rat race, just as we had earlier when we'd departed Fuji House. The lesson we were learning for a second time was that for foreigners residing in Tokyo who possessed the right social connections and enough disposable income, life could be very sweet indeed.

———

Time and again, we found that Tokyo's transit network was a great equalizer among the multitudes who rode it every day. All who entered did so at their own risk, considering the waves of commuters who descended into the elaborate, spidery network starting before sunrise to well past sunset. I remember well my first encounter with the Tokyo subway system just after arriving there as a graduate student. I was staying at one of the city's deluxe hotels located in the Akasaka section and participating in a cultural orientation program.

With a Canadian friend, I rode the elevator that steeply descended into the hubbub of Akasaka-Mitsuke Station, where four of Tokyo's most popular subway lines converge. This station was by no means the most crowded in Tokyo, but it seemed much busier than any I'd ever encountered in New York or elsewhere, even at rush hour. We walked over to the ticket-dispensing machine and faced a mind-boggling array of fare amounts and indecipherable, brightly illuminated Chinese characters indicating possible trip destinations. Having no idea what the fare might be to travel from Akasaka to Akihabara, the city's consumer electronics hub, we simply selected the lowest-price fare and headed towards the ticket wicket. Immediately, a blue-clad station employee in charge of clipping tickets began making unpleasant hand gestures and clicking sounds at us, clearly communicating that we'd made some grave error.

Barred from entering the train platforms and unable to determine what the correct price should be, we were on the verge of abandoning our travel plans when a solicitous young man explained to us in his politest halting English that we'd mistakenly purchased children's tickets. The station employee apparently thought we were trying to scam the system. Our Good Samaritan returned with us to the ticket machine and helped us purchase the correct adult fare and insert the proper yen coins into the machine. We were soon on our way, passing the ticket master with our heads held low, to avoid attracting his attention again.

Once we'd reached the platforms, we were relieved to see some of the signs in *romaji*, or Roman characters, indicating the destinations for each subway line. We chose the Ginza Line for our trip, which was then notorious for its inhumanely packed subway cars. We didn't know that at the time, of course. As the subway doors swung open, a torrent of overheated bodies spilled out onto the platform, nearly knocking us over in the process. We managed to dive out of the way at the last moment before being smothered by the commuter blob. We regained our footing and our composure, but by then the subway car was already at, or beyond, capacity. We decided to wait for another train to arrive.

This next time the doors swung open, we knew enough to stand clear and jump aboard just as the car emptied. The crowds behind us surged in with such force that we ended up pinned against the opposite door. Dave, a soft-spoken young man from rural Ontario, showed every sign of a full-fledged panic attack. He was silently sending me an

SOS, begging for release from our entrapment, when the doors swung open at the next stop, Toranomon Station. Another wave swept us out of the car and we managed to jump back on again just as the doors slammed closed. Back inside the car, we were both finding it difficult to gain purchase, as the many bodies compacted against us kept shifting. We seemed to be either stepping on someone's toes or elbowing someone in the head or making unwanted bodily contact with nearby passengers. My first instinct was to apologize to everyone I could, but nobody seemed to be responding or even particularly perturbed by our clumsiness. It seemed that this was just ordinary, everyday subway etiquette in Tokyo.

Arriving at Ginza Station, we disembarked from the Orange Ginza Line and went looking for the Grey Hibiya Line that would take us to Akihabara. We found it without too much difficulty and even grabbed two seats after boarding. We shook hands to congratulate ourselves for this remarkable feat. After riding this line for several minutes, we noticed that the train stations were getting farther and farther away from our intended destination. We disembarked just as soon as we could. With the help of a gaggle of schoolgirls, we got ourselves turned around in the right direction. We headed to the other side of the platform, but not without incurring peals of laughter each time we spoke to one of them in English. As we re-boarded the train, we smiled indulgently and waved our thanks to them for their support.

For the next several minutes, we took care to chart our progress at each subway stop, to be sure we were heading towards Akihabara Station. Upon arriving, we discovered many English-speaking foreigners who told us where to go for the best shopping. Akihabara was a kind of Disneyland for adult shoppers, with the latest, brightest, and most technologically-advanced electronic products on display at a wide variety of neon emporia that bustled with activity around the clock.

When Shelly and I first lived in Japan, groups of student friends had often traveled to Tokyo with the express purpose of visiting Akihabara to purchase the latest gadgets, while we would go see the sights of

Tokyo, party in the glitzy clubs of Roppongi. Finally, late at night, we would collapse onto hastily drawn-out *futon* mattresses for a short night's sleep at one of the city's cheaper *ryokan*, (traditional inns).

During those few times when we had lacked a Japanese friend to guide us, we'd sometimes boarded the wrong train. There seemed to be endless possibilities for traveling on the above-ground commuter lines, ranging from the *kakueki densha* (milk-run trains), to the *junkyuu* (limited expresses) and *kyuukoo* (express lines). Getting lost on them was simply a fact of life. It wasn't unusual to go speeding past our desired station when we'd only wanted to go one or two stops on the local train. Then we'd have to spend considerable time backtracking. Such were the lessons of trial and error on Tokyo's commuter train lines, until we'd finally become experts ourselves.

———

Domestic life in Tokyo as a married couple provided us with peace and stability, which served as a counterweight to the packed commuter trains that were a fact of our lives, along with our long hours of work and after-hours socializing. Our housing provided us with an oasis of privacy in a desert of urban hyper-development. Our landlords, the Saitos, had expanded what had been their modest single-family dwelling in Tokyo in the mid-20th century into a twelve-unit, six-story *mansion* (condominium) in the 1960s, around the time their family started to grow.

During the four years we lived in their building, their married adult son and daughter, along with their spouses and children, were living in the family compound. Mr. Saito's elderly mother was living there as well, having just recently lost her husband. Even in pricey, modern Tokyo, this family somehow managed to continue the extended-family traditions of Japan's past.

Mrs. Saito seemed to be everywhere during our sojourn there. In our early days, she was around to explain how the electricity worked, loaned us several kitchen appliances until we were able to purchase them, and offered constant tips about the neighborhood. She even helped us look for our cat when he escaped from the building one evening. She wandered around the neighborhood with us, calling out his name, until we found him hovering under a bush. A woman of unflappable poise and good-humor, she kept a close watch on our home and those of all the building residents.

Her husband often intimidated us with his gruff, even scowling, tone of voice. He limited his conversational exchanges to the bare minimum. His attention often seemed focused on plotting some new expansion project for the building. We later discovered that he was a talented performer of *Noh*, the traditional Japanese musical theater that involves stylized gestures with most communication done via finely crafted masks. His manner appeared to imitate his performance style. We took a while to learn how to read his subtle forms of communication.

We lived on the fifth floor for much of our time with them. The Saitos had designed a small artist's studio on the roof of the building, just a short walk up for us for the practice of *ikebana* (Japanese flower arranging), *shamisen* (the Japanese lute) or *cha no yu* (the tea ceremony). Adjoining this studio, they had lovingly crafted their miniature garden, replete with dwarf pines, a wide variety of flowering plants, a traditional Japanese lantern, and a picnic table and chairs carved from raw wood. We spent many enchanting hours on their roof, where the clang-clang of the nearby Yamanote line trains somehow blended nicely with the blooming of plum or cherry blossoms in the spring, hydrangeas and irises in summertime, and chrysanthemums in the fall. Our cat also used it as his place of escape from our cramped Tokyo digs.

In expensive and land-scarce Tokyo, the Saitos managed to live collectively, maintaining sacred family traditions. From the extensive contact we had with them, we never witnessed any cross words spoken. This family seemed to have successfully meshed the forces of maturity and youth, of continuity and unavoidable change, into their daily lives.

The smooth daily rhythm of life at home prompted me to reflect on the bunker mentality that I'd developed over the years living in large Western cities. In Tokyo, our building's main entrance downstairs remained unlocked twenty-four hours a day. Anyone could enter, although a stranger would have instantly been recognized as such by the building's residents. Mail was delivered to our individual mailboxes, which also remained unlocked in the lobby. We never had a reason to suspect that anything had been removed from them. We also never heard of any intruders breaking into any of the units.

This freedom from worry and crime was a distinguishing feature of our home life in those days and one we relished. Most foreign visitors to Tokyo were also struck by this blessed freedom of not having to think too much about personal safety. There were other problems that arose in Tokyo, of course, that would never have occurred in Western cities. For instance, it was not unusual for a Japanese door-to-door salesperson or deliveryman to fling open a customer's front door after only a cursory knock and announce his or her presence from the landing. In New York, such an action might have called for a retaliatory gun strike, but in Tokyo this practice was quite common. Salespeople generally had amicable and well-established relationships with their regular customers. They were frequent and accepted figures in the neighborhoods and knew the daily routines of the people in their territories.

———

Knowing and truly caring about one's neighbors had other benefits. Once when Shelly was traveling overseas, Mrs. Saito stopped by our apartment nearly every evening to check on me and invite me to dinner with her family. I accepted her kind invitation once and enjoyed their wonderful food and hospitality. Until Shelly returned, she continued to insist that I should dine with them. It would have been rude of me to accept too often, since the act of hosting me, a non-Japanese tenant, was trying for the family and disrupted their dining routines. It also would have been very easy for me to abuse their kindness, so I tactfully refused most of the invitations.

I learned from this episode that an older Japanese woman in Mrs. Saito's generation would find it virtually inconceivable that a married man could maintain a household in the absence of his wife. Such were the assumptions that shaped the constricted gender roles of domestic life in Japan—and still do, to a large extent. These deep-seeded perceptions about masculine ineptitude in the home stemmed from the imbalanced workaholic lives that many Japanese men had to endure to sustain the country's post-war economic miracle.

That miracle had lasted for four decades, from the early 1950s until the early 1990s, when the Japanese economy spiraled downward into a painful and seemingly unbreakable period of stagnation. This occurred towards the end of our stay in Japan. One of the sad side effects of the long period of self-sacrifice for Japanese fathers was that they ended up as virtual strangers in their own homes. They were often estranged from their children and sadly unfamiliar with the most basic daily activities in the household. For two generations, fathers had been seen mostly late at night and on Sundays.

Japanese male passivity and the lack of a consistent older male presence in the home long ago led to the curious relationship between many mothers and sons, in which mothers served as protectors for their vulnerable offspring during their formative years growing up and preparing intensively for the all-important college entrance examinations. In line with this special relationship, mothers performed all domestic chores that might conceivably distract the boys from their studies. Japan's fiercely competitive education system conforms to the Japanese preference for a meritocracy. Accordingly, those who study the longest and fiercest often pass the tough university exams and enter the most elite institutions.

Academic success, in turn, provides access to the most desirable Japanese employers, who nurture the newly hired, predominantly male employees as they progress from novices to executives in a choreographed progression. Ironically, with this system, the highly educated leaders of industry and government in Japan are often the least able to cope with the simplest domestic chores. The cycle repeats itself as large numbers of young men pattern their behavior on this model of strong mother and absent father. Therefore, domestic activities acquire a stigma in the eyes of most Japanese males; they consider them women's work that should be shunned at all cost.

Having married a little later than some of my peers, I had learned to manage cleaning, cooking, washing, and ironing. I listened with bemused interest to my Japanese male friends, who in all seriousness explained to me that work such as preparing the family budget, child rearing, and shopping, were intrinsically better suited to women. From my Western perspective, such attitudes that guaranteed my Japanese counterparts a free ride in the home smacked of extreme chauvinism.

One downside of this mindset was that by the time many executives had retired, they had acquired the dubious title of *gokibori dana* ("cockroach husband"), meaning they were always under foot when their frustrated wives least wanted them to be. I would have considered a lack of-participation in household activities as preventing me from controlling my own domestic affairs. Such differences of perception between the Japanese and me reveal the real differences in "small-c" culture that exist between East and West but aren't immediately apparent to a casual visitor. They strongly controlled the separation of work expectations and personal behaviors in Japanese homes.

———

Naturally, there were some negatives to domestic life and family activities in Tokyo. We were continuously surprised by the ability of many of our Japanese friends to screen out the ear-splitting noise that was a by-product of the city's widespread train system passing near most Tokyo apartments. Added to that were the interminable ringing of bells and alarms at these stations, the unending political announcements that blasted from the roofs of mobile vans operated by right-wing political operatives, and the screeching of bicycle brakes. We lived with pervasive noise for much of the day and night in Tokyo.

It was hard to fathom that this was the same place that venerated the serenity of nature. It was hard to imagine any Tokyoite possessing the haiku sensibilities of the poet Basho when he'd described a fine spring morn in 17th century Japan:

> *Listen! A frog*
> *Jumps into the stillness*
> *Of an ancient pond!*[12]

During our years in Tokyo, the rush of the reed, the trill of the cricket, and the gurgle of the carp were lost amid the racket created by throngs of school children, construction sites, and overhead rail lines. Even the most sublime venues—Ueno Park, Meiji Jingu Shrine and Shinjuku Imperials Gardens—suffered the tyranny of high-volume public service announcements. Tokyo wasn't the ideal spot for peaceful contemplation.

This had long been true. Even during the early 1900s Meiji era, for instance, the city was consumed by a frenzy of construction activities aimed at creating a modern city of commercial and residential buildings and a sophisticated tram system. The great Japanese novelist Natume Soseki referred to this in his masterly novel *Kokoro*: "Why one can say that in Tokyo today, there's not a moment of quiet, day or night."[13] That was still the case many decades later.

Of all the sources of the din that characterized Tokyo while we lived there, the most noticeable was the city's famed Yamanote circle line, which wound its way around the city for nearly twenty hours per day, beginning just after five o'clock in the morning, until its final trip well after midnight. This line has become part of the city's very soul, as evidenced by this selection from the popular book of *Tanka* poetry called *Salad Anniversary:*[14]

Spitting out the day's fatigue,
Taking it on again,
Round and round, it goes —
Evening train on the Yamanote Loop Line

The Japanese are noted for making the best of things, seeing the pro-verbial glass as half full rather than half empty. Some folks I talked to even went so far as to declare that they considered the sound of passing trains on this special line the very essence of Tokyo. How far removed that seemed from the melodious humming of the cicada or the plain-tive cry of the sweet potato vendor of yore! And yet, this very attitude seemed to sum up the resiliency we'd discovered among the Japanese we met during our time in Japan. The real allure of Tokyo stemmed from its extraordinary people, who worked and studied harder than their counterparts elsewhere. Tokyo was not the place for idlers or the faint of spirit.

———

Tokyo was—and still is—a city of myriad diversions and few ironclad rules for foreigners. Outside of egregious violations of public laws or morals, our hosts, showing bemused wonder, shrugged off most of our behavior. Rarely were we subject to direct criticism. Since all foreign-ers, no matter how long their stay in Japan, were considered temporary residents from the Japanese perspective, it was easy to play the role of the bewildered visitor long after we'd settled in and understood many of the unspoken rules. In this way, we could continue to enjoy the often-astonishing lengths the Japanese would go to in the name of in-ternational goodwill.

Many private English teachers, for instance, hardly ever paid for a meal out; they were regularly feted by their generous students. The same teachers would often receive extravagant gifts—gold watches, or-nate kimonos or beautifully crafted works of Chinese calligraphy—just for being teachers. How's that for appreciation? Being a *gaijin*, at least for those of us with North American or European pedigrees, meant receiving this type of preferential treatment and learning to be gracious about it. Nearly all of us were treated like media stars and were frequently invited to participate in TV programs, given free drinks at restaurants and coffee houses, and allowed to enter the most popular nightclubs free of charge. In general, we also lived in pricier lodgings than our Japanese counterparts. For those of us who happened to be especially outgoing or who craved the attention of a receptive audience, Tokyo was an ideal place to live. One survival guide for living in Japan described a key perk of being foreign there as having an opportunity to live in an environment where one is exposed to different values and ways of thinking.[15]

Even with the many perks we were enjoying, by the time we'd been in Tokyo for five years, Shelly and I both knew it was time to move on. At that point, we were both feeling the burnout that comes when one's engines have been firing on all cylinders for too long. Not only had we been working long hours in our respective Japanese offices, we'd also been building a successful consulting business catering to Japanese corporations and individuals.

Our business had pretty much sprung up in our final two years without much planning on our part. It happened to several other expatriates we knew who'd survived the initial winnowing out process while living in Tokyo. After a few years, resident *gaijin* begin to comprehend how things work in Japan and to speak the language serviceably. In that way, they start to have a real talent for serving as cultural bridges between East and West.

In the early 1990s, many of Japan's leading enterprises were relocating significant numbers of local executives to North America, Europe, and Australia as part of the country's effort to lower production costs by establishing principal manufacturing facilities in key overseas markets. As our network of professional and personal contacts had expanded, we were often invited to bid on pre-departure training projects, to prepare Japanese officers for overseas duty. Projects of this sort were lucrative in yen compensation, but they required our considerable time and effort to prepare the training materials, lead the days-long training sessions, and write post-training reports. We were discovering that the line between our work and personal spaces had long since melted away. We were eager to re-establish it, if we could.

Both of us were also feeling the tug of our consciences, wanting to do work that better served humanity rather than just training individuals to communicate in English and function overseas. Not to say that those weren't important skills, but we hoped to go even deeper into other cultures and other service-oriented activities. We had both spent a fair number of years in high-pressure cities in the developed world, and we started to consider ways to live and work in a developing world situation that would represent a complete change of direction.

We started applying for work at development and charitable organizations, sending out feelers and job applications to Oxfam, Care, World Vision, and Save the Children, among others. In many ways, the requirements for working at any of these non-profits were as rigorous, if not more so, than in private-sector jobs. We also faced many of the same challenges to prove that we had the credentials and dedication needed to succeed in a totally new line of work. Shelly was finally able to break through in an unexpected way. She was offered a U.S. Peace Corps training officer position in Bangkok, which seemed to offer us a way to recalibrate her skills and redirect our lifestyle.

She had previously worked in the non-profit world for a U.S.-Japan grassroots organization in the Washington D.C. area. She'd also trained many Japanese clients. This background made a positive impression on the Peace Corps hiring officials in Washington. Shelly got an offer for a job that was scheduled to begin soon. Ready for a new adventure, we decided that the timing, the location, and the opportunity for growth were just about right. After a memorable week of pre-service training in the Philippines, we returned to Tokyo to pack our things. Our incredible, eye-opening sojourn in Japan was about to end. Before long we were on our way to Bangkok for the next stop on our cross-cultural odyssey.

2: Bangkok, Thailand

Pid Tong Lang Pra – A Thai Proverb
(Do good deeds without seeking attention for them.)

Bangkok is an unforgettable city. Nowadays it ranks right at, or near, the top of lists of preferred travel destinations. That wasn't the case in the early 1990s, when we arrived there. At that time, it was widely considered to be a hardship location rife with political dissent and serious air pollution. It's quite probable that Shelly and I were able to relocate there expressly for those reasons. Many Americans were reluctant to live in Bangkok, which reduced the competition for international jobs in Thailand. After our Tokyo interlude, we were eager to explore a different kind of Asian culture. Bangkok seemed to be just the ticket.

Indeed, Thailand turned out to be a real contrast with Japan. Consider the country we encountered in the spring of 1993. The Thai government had just installed a new prime minister who was a member of the minority Democratic Party. He was widely perceived as a compromise leader in response to the protracted and violent street demonstrations that had rocked Bangkok a year earlier. The city was still reeling from this popular uprising against a heavy-handed and unpopular military leader. Thailand's revered monarch, King Bhumipol IX, had convinced the brutish general and the leaders of the grassroots student movement to sit down together and had told them in no uncertain terms to stop the street fighting. Thailand was going to transition to new and peaceful elections.

In those days, the word of the Thai king was unquestioned. His highness was still in vigorous health, wielding a moral authority that united much of the country. At his urging, the main parties in the dispute did cease and desist and called for new elections. Nevertheless, the city's international reputation as a hot spot lingered on. Many wondered how long the new Thai government would survive.

After departing Tokyo one chilly April morning, we arrived in sunny Bangkok several hours later. We experienced an immediate and powerful sensory switch: from temperate Japan to tropical Thailand. Stepping from the exit doors at Don Muang International Airport in the north of Bangkok, we were struck by a blast of hot, humid air combined with the dust of unimaginable numbers of automobiles, taxis, motorbuses, and noisy three-wheeled vehicles called *tuk-tuks*. April is the peak month in Thailand's scorching dry season, when temperatures soar. That year was no exception. In addition, the cacophony of sounds pummeling us from all directions wasn't something we'd expected. We steeled ourselves against the roar of heavy trucks from the overhead highway and the persistent honking of heavy traffic gridlock.

In short order, we had our first exposure to the staccato rhythm and sharp, musical tones of the Thai language. *Bai nai farang*? ("Where are you going, foreigner?") inquired a nearby idler. We weren't sure where we'd be heading at that moment. We'd been told that an official driver from the U.S. Peace Corps would be waiting for us there at the airport. Just then, a polite-looking man in gray pants and a short-sleeved blue work shirt stepped towards us and asked in hesitant English if we were the newly arrived Peace Corps couple. We answered in the affirmative, and he escorted us past the hawker, up a ramp to a nearby parking structure, and into the cool comfort of a dark, air-conditioned sedan. The contrast in temperatures was shocking, but we soon relished the drier, chilled air.

As our sedan wound its way through several intersecting byways and eventually merged onto an overhead expressway, we had our introduction to a traffic-choked city in mid-afternoon. Much of the infrastructure that now defines the dynamic Thai capital was either still in its early design stages or under construction. The city resembled a construction zone. Pylons for what would become the overhead sky train were under construction; it now bisects the busy city. The Suvarnabhumi Second Bangkok International Airport, located east of town, handles most of the city's air traffic nowadays; when we arrived, it was still on the drawing board. Many of the high-speed expressways that wind their way through the huge metropolis were only partially completed. You could enter them, but you wouldn't go far before you were diverted onto a dusty side street.

What we experienced along the way into the city was a jerky, stop-and-start motion along the partially completed Don Muang Airport Expressway. Our stomachs lurched forward and backward with each pounding of the brakes by our clumsy driver. The vehicle's tinted glass provided us with a brief glimpse of the large Chatuchak public market sprawl mid-city as we sped by it, as well as the muddy Chao Phraya River as we crossed over it on one of Bangkok's scenic bridges. Below, we could see the busy river taxis and barges that appeared to be transporting the city's residents and foodstuffs, as well as other raw materials from docks farther up river.

We finally arrived at our destination, a modern hotel that was to be our new home for our first week in Thailand. Located in Thonburi, an old historic center on the west bank of the Chao Phraya, it was away from most of the popular tourist spots, which are on the other side. The hotel was modest by Bangkok standards, mostly glass and chrome on the outside and heavily air-conditioned on the inside. It provided just the basic amenities budget-conscious travelers to Thailand require: a small room with twin beds and a basic European-style breakfast each morning. This setting was appropriate, considering we were now affiliated with the U.S. Peace Corps. We would have to readjust to living in a simpler way than what we had been enjoying during our final few years in Tokyo. We'd soon be interacting with American volunteers who would be living in even simpler accommodations. From the start, we were meant to be role models for the volunteers who had been placed throughout all of Thailand's different geographic regions in the north, northeast, center, eastern coast and south of the country. They, in turn, would be emulating the lifestyles of their Thai counterparts.

———•———

Daily life in Bangkok was educational. It featured a rich Buddhist culture deeply rooted in Southeast Asian history, but with strong Indian influences, too. The beliefs and rituals of millions of adherents of Thailand's sect of Theravada Buddhism were on public display. Their practices were meant to imitate those performed by the Buddha thousands of years ago on the Indian sub-continent. For instance, Thai monks in their Saffron robes lived the humble lifestyle prescribed by Buddha, shaving their heads and walking the streets with bowls in hand each morning, as they begged for food and alms. This was as normal in Bangkok as it was in the villages we'd soon be visiting upcountry.

After becoming acquainted with the more austere hands-off approach of Japanese Buddhist sects, we soon realized that the Thai version profoundly affected most Thais, and Thai monks played an active role in their society. Thai Prime Minister Chuan Leekpai often expressed pride in his education at a Buddhist temple school. This was the norm for boys who came from families of modest means. Leekpai was an exception, though, as most other Thai prime ministers hailed from long-established and wealthy Thai families.

As is true for all religions, Thai Buddhism has its dark side. It experienced its share of the scandals and temptations so endemic in the human condition. While we were living in Bangkok, and during our later visits to Thailand for our graduate school research, one or two Thai temples were always the focus of public scrutiny, due to their unorthodox fund-raising schemes, vast wealth, and their abbots' luxurious lifestyles. While most monks used public donations for educational and charitable purposes and to maintain their temple grounds, a small minority couldn't resist self-aggrandizement, even hedonism.

Our transition to Thailand was especially challenging for me, as I was suddenly on an extended sabbatical from my previous work as a writer and editor. Having become accustomed to working hard according to the Japanese mindset, I now had to dramatically downshift to a slower pace of life as I tried to decide what to pursue next. Shelly had a clear description of what would be expected of her. For me, the time ahead was a total blank in terms of what I'd be doing and where I'd be working. At least, that was how I perceived things at first.

This new start didn't mean that I'd lack things to do, especially for the first several weeks in country. We began meeting Shelly's new colleagues, moving into our new home, and undergoing Thai culture and language orientation. Everyone who has been through this kind of official posting knows how important protocols are. Making a good impression on your host-country counterparts sets the tone, not only for a good working relationship, but it also puts your best foot forward as an overseas representative of your country.

In Thailand, this settling-in process was magnified by the sensitivities of the Thai people, who expected white-collar employees to present themselves in a way they called *riproi*, or polished and well-clad even at the hottest of times. After the cool weather in Japan, we were sweltering, but we had to dress in our usual attire for work: jacket, blouse, and skirt for Shelly; jacket, shirt, and tie for me. Within a matter of a few weeks, though, we were able to modify this garb to a more informal but still *riproi* cotton blouse and linen skirt combo for Shelly and batik shirt and pressed khaki pants for me.

During that hot season, we constantly craved water and air-conditioning—in roughly equal portions. The lovely historic mansion that housed the U.S. Peace Corps staff provided both. In fact, the facilities were over-air conditioned, which is something we discovered that many Thais prefer. This meant we'd have to bring a sweater or jacket to work to ward off the cold office environment. While I wasn't formally employed at that point, I was still able to use the Peace Corps library to job hunt and read more about the Thai culture. I also joined in Shelly's language and training activities that were intended to ease our transition. It was heartening to see that Peace Corps administrators and staff were sensitive to family members and the positive impact training could have on the morale of their American employees. Most of the Thai staff were fluent in American English, gracious of manner, and solicitous towards us during our period of cultural transition. Many had been with the Peace Corps since its earliest days in Thailand, in the 1960s, and had advanced professionally. By the 1990's, many of these Thai employees were approaching a well-deserved retirement.

At that time and throughout our nearly three years there, the U.S. Peace Corps in Thailand was at its historic peak in terms of volunteers in service. Approximately two hundred Americans were serving there, with an annual intake and outflow of around ninety volunteers. The breadth of training programs was extensive. Not only did the volunteers do a three-month intensive language and cultural training program after arrival, but they also participated in a technical training program tailored to their area of expertise. These included elementary education, public health, HIV/AIDS prevention, national parks, fisheries, integrated pest management, and others.

While Shelly was striving to get up to speed as one of the two Peace Corps training managers, she was also studying Thai with one of her *kruu* (language teachers). I joined in as often as I could. It was clear to me that the Peace Corps approach to language teaching and learning was different from any other training methodologies I'd encountered before. Peace Corps language trainers mostly worked to foster communicative competence and self-confidence among their American volunteer students. Language was intended for real-world situations that the volunteers would encounter at site. Such competence could be described as the ability to use the language correctly and appropriately to accomplish communication goals. According to proponents of this approach, the desired outcome of language learning was to communicate competently, *not* necessarily with the ability to use the language exactly as a native speaker does.[16]

Thai language trainers focused more on developing volunteer speaking and listening skills in Thai rather than on their reading and writing abilities. They assumed the volunteers would need to be comprehensible in their villages and able to comprehend their counterparts' spoken words. Relatively less training time was spent on learning the Thai alphabet, which was complex and derived from Sanskrit.

We normally met with our *kruu*, a dedicated young Thai lady with a very understated and affable manner, around mid-afternoon on a shaded outdoor terrace just outside Shelly's Peace Corps office. We sat on a rattan sofa with batik design cushions, and our teacher sat opposite us in a padded rattan chair. A slowly oscillating overhead ceiling fan generated a gentle breeze to cool us off.

Our first few lessons were dedicated to acquiring survival Thai. In our first lesson, we learned that Thai men and women ended their sentences with differing words – *kaa* for women and *krup* for men, to sound polite. Women were expected to pronounce the terminal syllable in a high tone of voice and men in a low tone. The resulting sounds were very much like the sound made by a blackbird (caw!) for women and the sound made when angry (crap!) for men.

We also reviewed the five vocal tones associated with Thai: mid, high, low, rising, and falling, which were like Chinese Mandarin tones. This isn't surprising, considering that nearly half of the population of Bangkok is of Chinese origin and has been for many years.[17] Thai's multi-tonal nature causes embarrassment for unpracticed foreigners and even for Thais themselves, because mispronounced words lead to wildly different meanings from what was intended. For instance, the Thai word *ma* means horse when said with a middle tone. If you say it with a falling tone, it means mother. To our untrained ears, the difference in sounds was a subtle one, but we caused some laughs when trying out these new sounds in public.

Considering the possibility of miscommunication, it would have been easy to become paranoid about saying even the slightest thing in Thai. Fortunately, most Thais seemed to have endless fun with the language we produced and were kind enough to forgive foreigners for our slips of the tongue or vocal cords. They expected us to say goofy things—and we didn't disappoint them in that regard. The main point of communication in Thailand seemed to be to have a good time (*tam sanuk*). I found that while I couldn't quite capture the cadences of rising or falling tones correctly, most Thais were more than willing to try and decipher my efforts, provided I laughed right along with them. Another aspect I enjoyed of Thai language and culture was the widespread use of nicknames. I was quickly given the nickname *Sung* (said in a middle tone), which means tall.

Our teachers and colleagues were generally known more by their nicknames than their family names, which were often very long and hard to remember. Young teachers might call one another *Bu* ("Crab"), *Ooan* ("Fattie"), *Daeng* ("Red"), and so on, based on their most obvious personal characteristics. Nobody seemed to take any offense; on the contrary, most Thais relished the chance to feel closer to one another in this funny way. It made Thai language studies less intimidating, since we could be studying the language and practicing new conversation with a teacher named *Lek* ("Small").

———

Another thing we needed to learn right away was the use of the honorific title *Khun* with other adults. This title encompassed all Western titles—Mr., Mrs., or Miss—and signified respect towards another adult. Unlike Westerners, Thais used *Khun* followed by your first name, not your last name. Khun Jeff, for example, was my title and name. This allowed us to avoid pronouncing complicated, multi-syllabic Thai family names and the Thais could avoid using Western family names that were hard to pronounce.

As in other Asian cultures, Thais showed respect towards the elderly—and, in fact, toward any person older than themselves. The use of the words *Pi* (older person) and *Nong* (younger person) acknowledged one's status in the Thai hierarchy. A *Pi* was expected to support a *Nong* while a *Nong* was expected to defer to the greater knowledge of a *Pi*. This was as true in professional life as it was in personal encounters. We couldn't take this all in right away, of course. It took many months before we started applying these principles in daily life. The value of seniority represented a cultural logic that slowly unfolded as we met many Thais of diverse backgrounds and learned to behave appropriately.

In our early days in Bangkok, we depended on Peace Corps staff, trainers, and other acquaintances to serve as our cultural intermediaries and mentors. We were also very fortunate to attend a speech given by an experienced Thailand hand, William Klausner, who spoke to a new group of American volunteers. A native New Yorker, Klausner had originally come to Thailand in the 1950s on a Ford Foundation Fellowship and had remained there for several decades. His book *Reflections on Thai Culture* was a great resource for Westerners living in Thailand. Many appreciate his insights even today.[18] Klausner provided useful and amusing anecdotes about his early experiences in a traditional Isan village in northeast Thailand. He also provided his perspective on contemporary social changes and how things worked in Thailand's increasingly urban society.

The volunteers, Shelly, and I listened with rapt attention and respect for a man who had clearly internalized both Western and Eastern values and could describe them both so well. Klausner discussed the changing gender roles of Thai couples. Traditionally, Thai women were perceived metaphorically as occupying the hindquarters of the elephant, with Thai men in the front. What he was saying was that Thai males enjoyed clear advantages over females in the social hierarchy. In daily life, for instance, most Thai men had the option of becoming monks in their youth and "making merit", accumulating good karma for themselves and their families. This placed nearly all men on a strong footing within the firmament of Thai society, since their good works were widely recognized and appreciated.

Thai women, on the other hand, were expected to handle much of the daily grunt work: feeding and cleaning the monks at the temples and managing and supporting their own families. Thai women were expected to serve as workhorses, while Thai men could enjoy being show horses. Women had to labor hard and long from early adulthood onward. Men, in contrast, were often expected to do good deeds in their youth and then to represent their families nobly by studying hard and, they hoped, working for the government or a large company one day.

It was impossible for Klausner to skirt the topic of Thailand's notorious sex industry, so he dove right in. All of us were interested in discussing the causes of sex work and why it was tolerated so widely in Thai society. Klausner shared with us how surprised he had been by the casual attitude of Thai males toward sex workers. He said that his Thai male friends used to treat an outing to a local brothel like young Western males treat an afternoon at a good action movie. For Thai men, there didn't seem to be any stigma attached to visiting sex workers. This was plain to see any night, judging by the large crowds in popular bars, strip shows, and brothels in Bangkok's red-light districts near Patpong Road and Soi Cowboy. A sizeable proportion of visitors were Western and Japanese male tourists, and even some Western women.

Our time in Bangkok occurred in the mid 1990s, just a few years after AIDS had exploded as a public health crisis in Thailand and Southeast Asia. Thai attitudes towards sex gradually changed as the country came to grips with the rising number of stricken adults. Sexual mores and behaviors were discussed more often in schools and even in the workplace. Community activists included Senator Meechai Viravaidya, better known as Mr. Condom. He had begun distributing free or low-cost condoms to bars, restaurants, and nightclubs linked to the sex industry. Local parades and parties featured speeches about healthy sexual roles and practices and ended with a distribution of condoms.

Many dedicated Peace Corps volunteers had developed youth and community health-related educational materials in English and Thai and were distributing these wherever they could, even in the most hard-core areas of Bangkok's sex industry. Their efforts, along with those of many health-related non-governmental organizations, were still in full force a decade later when we returned to Thailand for field research. Later, our focus as academics would be on Thai anti-trafficking and poverty-reduction projects, and our field research would include interviews with community organizers, some of whom were targeting the country's sex workers, and on-site observations.

————

After we'd been in Bangkok for a week, Peace Corps administrators notified us that our staff housing was available. We were excited to pack up our belongings, including our two cats, and make the trek to our new home. Our Peace Corps driver loaded our many bags carefully into the agency's station wagon. We headed back across the Chao Phraya River to our new neighborhood in the Dusit area of town. This district is best known for the exquisitely crafted Teakwood palace used by the Thai royal family.

Our new place was in a private compound a few miles from the Peace Corps Thailand office. As we drove in, the guard smiled politely and motioned us towards a bridge that passed over a small *klong*, or canal, which intersected the property. The expatriate residents living in the compound all had their own Thai-style homes, two-story concrete structures embellished with attractive ceiling trims and teakwood verandas. The location impressed us as a private haven removed from the hubbub of the Bangkok street traffic just outside.

As we approached our new home, a petite Thai woman came forward and introduced herself as Teem. She was our housekeeper and cook during our stay in Bangkok. Khun Teem had a personal story that we found to be common among poor Thai laborers living in Bangkok. She had migrated to the big city several years earlier from her village near Udorn Thani in Isan, the region in northeast Thailand that is characterized by a large arid plain. It occupies nearly one-third of Thailand's

land mass. In those years and beyond, it was becoming increasingly untenable for its large population to live there, and most Thais leaving
Isan headed straight to Bangkok, whose population ballooned to over
eight million people.[19]

A relative or friend from her native village had some years earlier
introduced Khun Teem to a U.S. Peace Corps official. From then onward, she had worked for a succession of Peace Corps families. We were
her third or fourth American employer. Our immediate Peace Corps
predecessor, a single American woman, had formed a close bond with
her, paid for her English language lessons, and encouraged her to speak
English in the house. That same lady had supported Teem in building a
small bakery business on the side, to supplement her family's income.
Thanks to our predecessor's kindnesses, not only could Teem speak
English at a basic level, she could also prepare Western dishes such as
quiche, salads (not much favored by Thais), and even brownies. Things
were looking very promising for us.

We soon discovered that Teem had been living with her husband
and teenaged daughter adjacent to our home, in what was essentially
a lean-to room intended for one domestic servant. All the homes in
our compound had been constructed with the assumption that one
housekeeper would be thrilled to have such lodgings. Owing to the dire
situation in Isan and the high cost of accommodations in Bangkok, impoverished migrant workers would end up sharing close quarters like
this one with family members. Everyone was grateful to have a clean
and safe place to lay their heads.

Another surprise awaited us on our very first morning there. As we
were eating breakfast, Teem and her adolescent daughter entered the
house and sat and chatted amiably together on our living room sofa.
It appeared that they had been allowed to enter and leave our house
whenever they wanted. This was awkward, since Shelly and I valued
our privacy and expected to have some quiet time before the onslaught
of conversation on workdays. We wondered how to explain to her that
we didn't want to interact directly with them so early in the morning.

The issue was cultural, the concept of personal privacy, which didn't translate easily into the Thai mindset. Like other collectivist societies in Asia, Thai culture is geared towards a communal lifestyle, with the preeminence of groups such as families or companies overshadowing the needs of individuals. The concept of an individual having time alone would not occur to many Thais unless they had spent extended time in the West.

We turned to Shelly's assistant at the Peace Corps, Khun Alisa, to act as our cultural intermediary. She said she'd explain to Khun Teem about the importance of privacy to many Americans. Alisa had lived in the U.S. and had years of experience working with American volunteers in Thailand. She knew how many volunteers cherished private time for recharging their mental batteries. She informed Khun Teem that henceforth she should arrive for work after we'd departed the house and that she should limit the time her daughter spent there, especially when we were at home. Khun Teem seemed to take this in stride, but her daughter never really warmed to us after that.

It was strange being at home so much more than I'd ever been in Tokyo or the U.S. In those pre-internet days, it wasn't possible to log onto your desktop or laptop computer and entertain yourself with videos, social media, or interesting web links. Instead, you were pretty much confined to reading books or magazines or watching television. Fortunately, we'd received a terrific resource guide with our orientation materials for new members of the U.S. mission in Thailand. The *Bangkok Guide*[20] provided a huge amount of useful information for sightseeing, shopping, and traveling in the Bangkok metropolitan area; it even advised on ways to network with the many professional organizations in town.

As a former working journalist and member of the Foreign Correspondents' Club in Tokyo, I was eager to get involved with its counterpart in Bangkok. What I discovered was that the Bangkok club was far less active than the one in Tokyo. Its agenda included only one or two activities per month, contrasting markedly with the Tokyo club, which had been a hub of activity, scheduling many events every week. So much for using my press credentials in Bangkok.

To acclimate myself as much as I could to the local scene, I used the *Bangkok Guide* and the accompanying illustrated map of Bangkok by Nancy Chandler[21] to plan daytrips for myself in my new hometown. Many Peace Corps volunteers swore by Chandler's map for discovering the most fascinating places in the city. The tricky part was to make myself understood by drivers of taxis or *tuk-tuks*, the three-wheeled motorized rickshaws that zoomed all over Bangkok day and night. The Chandler map had colorful drawings of most of the tourist hotspots. While I did my best to sound out my desired locations phonetically, I often had to resort to pointing to my destination.

My favorite outing was to hop on a *tuk-tuk* or to go on foot to the closest Chao Phraya River dock; these served as the point of entry for boarding the city's many water taxis, which transported thousands every day up and down the river. Considering Bangkok's notorious traffic, it was the best way to get around the city. Fortunately, many of the most alluring spots were conveniently located along the riverbanks.

I always marveled at the magnificent sight of *Wat Arun*, the Temple of the Dawn, which towered over the west bank of the Chao Phraya. Nearly opposite it, on the other side of the river, was the absolute focal point of the old city: the splendid architectural gem called *Wat Phra Kaew*. This has served as the traditional Grand Palace, where the Emerald Buddha has long been venerated. For a recently arrived American, these places were as close to the exotic Orient as I could ever have imagined. It was entirely possible to roam around these monuments in a state of total bewilderment and awe if I so desired. Eventually, though, the formidable heat on most days would force me to move on, in search of shade and beverages.

Traveling south down the Chao Phraya River, I passed Yaowarat, the city's Chinatown district, then a string of Bangkok five-star hotels, including the Bangkok Sheraton, the Shangri-La, and the world-famous Oriental Hotel Bangkok, which, for years, was ranked as the world's best hotel. Stopping for lunch at the Oriental early on in our stay, Shelly and I immediately understood its appeal. The quarters were immaculate in every way, from the spacious lobby that afforded a bright, uncluttered view of the passing river traffic to the elegantly-attired staff finely trained in welcoming guests in many languages. Upon entering the hotel, we were instantly transported into an environment of gracious hospitality and unstinting comfort.

The hotel took a dim view of visitors who weren't property dressed or behaved. Several years earlier, when we were living in Tokyo, Shelly and I had taken a trip to Bangkok during Japan's annual "golden week" of holidays, which is celebrated in late April and early May. We were younger and not yet serving as official representatives of the U.S. government when we spent the day sightseeing along the Chao Phraya River before stopping at the Oriental Hotel's dock. We were dressed in the typical sightseers' outfits—shorts and a khaki shirt for me; a skirt and colorful cotton blouse for Shelly; sandals for both of us.

As we strolled up the steps leading to the main entrance of the hotel, we were approached by one of the hotel's security representatives, who informed us in no uncertain terms that we weren't welcome at the hotel in such attire. This was our first and only banishment from any establishment in Bangkok, or in all of Thailand, for that matter. We, as whites, were afforded no special treatment regarding the hotel's dress code, which wasn't the case in many other such establishments in Bangkok. At the time, though, it served as an important reminder that places still existed that were intended only for the use of persons of a certain rank, and it was clear we hadn't achieved that rank yet.

This time around, we were not underdressed or barred entry from the Oriental. I wore a linen jacket and pressed shirt, and Shelly wore a Thai silk tailored outfit. The doormen warmly greeted us and ushered us in with pleasant smiles. We strode through the elegantly decorated lobby to the hotel's cheerful riverfront coffee shop, which afforded us an unparalleled view and a very nice menu selection of Thai and Western dishes.

As it was our first time to dine there, we both opted for Thai main courses. Shelly went for the *pad thai*, Thailand's ever-popular noodle dish, made with peanuts and prawns. I chose to be a little more adventurous, selecting a red curry chicken dish with rice. The menu indicated that this was a spicy dish, and I had my water glass poised nearby at the ready. Spicy proved to be an understatement. I bit into what appeared to be baby carrots, but they were, in fact, Thai hot peppers coated in garlic sauce. Within seconds, tears were streaming down my face. Downing half a glass of water didn't help lessen the fiery flavor.

Signaling my distress to our waiter with panicked cries, he quickly ran over and explained to us that white rice was a better fire extinguisher than water. After devouring several heaping spoons of rice, it was clear he was right. My mouth started to return to its normal temperature, although my lips tingled for several minutes more. I finally shoved my plate aside, called our bemused waiter back, and requested another plate of non-spicy *pad thai* from him. That would be my meal that day and for many meals onward, until my taste buds adjusted to Thai spices. Thereafter we'd frequently ask waiters, friends, or whoever might be dining nearby just how hot an unfamiliar dish was.

———

After a few weeks of exploring the many treasures Bangkok had to offer, including the Jim Thompson Teak House, Lumpini Park, the Erawan Shrine, and several public markets, I began to grow restless, fully aware that I should get back to some type of gainful employment. Considering my limited knowledge of Thai, there weren't many jobs I could find in the local economy. Reporting or editing would be difficult to pursue because much of the communication with local contacts had to be done in Thai.

The Peace Corps network of staff, American volunteers, and contractors was well established. Through them, I heard about a potential job opportunity. One of the American trainers for new volunteers had recently been teaching at Mahidol University, one of the leading institutions of higher education in the country. This university had a downtown campus in Bangkok known for its medical school and a newer, fast-growing suburban campus located west of Bangkok. This newer campus was offering college-level courses in English and periodically needed native instructors to fill teaching slots. My contact introduced me to the staff member who hired new instructors and before long I was designing a new curriculum in Entrepreneurship. I would be teaching forty undergraduate students.

I fell into this teaching work rather than planning for it. In Tokyo, most of my teaching experience had involved either private school English courses or individualized programs for Japanese executives going abroad. This time, I'd be teaching a course for business majors. These students needed to demonstrate intermediate or higher-level proficiency in English to enroll in this program. The school's English language teachers were responsible for training and testing them and for certifying that they could pursue all their studies in English.

There was a certain irony in the fact that I'd been chosen to teach these students and this class. For one thing, it was immediately apparent from day one that my students were from the cream of the crop of Thai society. One look at the school parking lot where scores of Mercedes, BMWs, and Land Rovers were parked confirmed that many came from money. Their clothes, shoes, hairstyles, and jewelry all declared that they were dressing for success. As the students took turns introducing themselves, most described prior travel to the U.S., Canada, or Europe. Many also spoke of their families' businesses, which elicited a knowing murmur from their fellow students. Upon graduating, many would inherit executive positions at cement companies, agribusinesses, garment factories, and other manufacturing operations.

The chance of these students starting their own small businesses seemed slim, considering these family connections. I wondered exactly what my purpose was in teaching them. As a saving grace, a minority—maybe twenty percent—were attending classes on scholarships and might benefit from the course content. It was towards these students, from the middle or lower-middle class, that I remained the most sensitive during my teaching stint. They tended to remain reserved in class and had to be encouraged to speak up.

I'd never been an entrepreneur and knew little about the logistics of operating a small enterprise, but it was clear to me that my students had even less knowledge. Before the days of the internet, I turned to my parents for help in generating teaching materials, asking them to send me back issues of *Success, Money,* and *Fortune* magazines, among others. I was also able to cobble together parts of my old MBA textbooks on management, operations, marketing, and accounting for a serviceable curriculum.

As a new instructor without a teaching assistant to support me, I was saddled with all the paperwork associated with the course. I also had to make copies of handouts for all my students, which was harder than it might seem, since there was only one working copier in the business department and it was well used. I spent much of my time before or after class staking my claim to the copier. My keenest memory of that summer course is of incessant grading. With forty students required to do a research report, complete a mid-term test, make a project presentation, and take a final comprehensive exam, I was always lugging a large satchel of student papers home. I'd then spend much of the next two days grading them before toting them back again to school.

I was teaching the children of the haves in Thai society while Shelly and the Peace Corps volunteers were working upcountry in Thai villages with the have-nots. These volunteers included a new cohort of forty-five Americans who had arrived in Thailand just a few weeks after we had. At the onset of their stay, the volunteers had spent a week in Bangkok receiving various welcomes by the senior Peace Corps staff, as well having medical tests done and reviewing materials related to their tours of duty.

After this orientation, they'd been shifted to two rural training sites on Thailand's eastern coast, not too far from Cambodia. There they'd received the normal three months of specialized, pre-service training, much of it in village settings like the actual locations where they would do their service. I was impressed by the diversity of volunteer ages, from twenty-two to seventy-two, and their determination to plunge right in and live as Thai villagers live. As the person responsible for the development and delivery of their training sessions, Shelly had to be there on site for a good amount of the three months, to oversee everything. Like all incoming Peace Corps volunteer cohorts, this one graduated at an elaborate close-of-training ceremony in Bangkok, which featured the participation of the U.S. Ambassador to Thailand and inspiring speeches by Thai government officials and Peace Corps volunteers. In the days that followed, the volunteers were shipped off to their permanent work sites for their term of in-country service.

My teaching schedule allowed me time to make occasional visits to the training site and to attend the closing ceremony. In many ways, my situation wasn't too different from that of the volunteers. Although I was teaching affluent Thai young people who traveled to school in luxury sedans, I fended for myself on public transport. My regular route took me from our compound to the university campus an hour west of Bangkok near the Thai provincial town of Nakorn Pathom.

Shelly and I hadn't been able to purchase a private vehicle of our own. She was allotted a Peace Corps vehicle for work use and drove it frequently. I had to get to school however I could. I discovered that the best way to get to Mahidol University was on an express bus that departed several blocks from our home. It headed directly west across the Krung Thon bridge spanning the Chao Phraya River and into the thick scrub of the Thai countryside. It stopped abruptly at various rural outposts along the way before reaching its destination near the university entrance.

One challenge for me was the bus's schedule. It stopped once per hour at the designated spot near our home and occasionally it arrived late. As my course started at ten o'clock in the morning, I had to board the eight o'clock bus, rather than the nine o'clock, to ensure I wouldn't be late. The express bus was air-conditioned, which was not the case for the packed local buses. I felt so lucky to travel in climate-controlled conditions because local temperatures were steamy even at that early hour. Without the express bus comfort, I would have arrived at my class a rumpled mess.

What I learned from this teaching adventure was that an individual's status was critical both within Thai society and within its academic culture. Although an American colleague had introduced me to the Thai staff at Mahidol, I hadn't previously known any of the Thai faculty members. To the Thais I probably resembled just another temporary American educator who would stay for just one term before leaving. Indeed, that is exactly what happened. Had I come to Mahidol with a full range of academic credentials and high-level faculty backing, as I did several years later in other educational settings, very likely I would have enjoyed more resources than I needed, including my own office and a staff member as a mentor. In those circumstances, I would likely have stayed longer and taught additional courses.

To be honest, while I valued the challenge of teaching, I had entered university teaching prematurely and felt overwhelmed by the workload. It included developing new course materials; deciding on an appropriate teaching method for my highly confident students; managing the class in an unfamiliar, cross-cultural setting; and evaluating their course assignments in fair and appropriate ways. These are skills I'd acquire later, during our Los Angeles years, when Shelly and I pursued graduate degrees in international education at the University of Southern California. But that occurred long after I taught this class. In Bangkok, I was teaching by instinct, grit, and humor, with just a dash of cultural sensitivity thrown in.

———•———

Shortly after completing the Mahidol course, I started searching for a job inside the U.S. mission that might be more suitable for me. By now, the thought of a normal desk job in a Western-style office building with English-speaking employees seemed very attractive. Bangkok has been described as the hottest city on earth in terms of average annual temperature[22], and it certainly felt that way to me that year. My teaching stint took place during the long monsoon season that begins in June and reaches a crescendo of heavy thunderstorms and stifling heat by September or October. I was ready to stay out of the heat as much as possible.

One day, while flipping through a recent issue of *About Bangkok*, the weekly newsletter of the U.S. Embassy in Thailand, I zeroed in on a job advertisement for the position of Community Liaison Officer. This job appeared to be a catchall that involved meeting with embassy newcomers, providing them with information and coping strategies for living in Bangkok, getting their kids registered at local international schools, offering tips on available jobs to spouses, and organizing U.S. Mission special events. This job is normally offered to an eligible spouse of a U.S. government official working in the country.

I felt I had a good chance of nailing it, considering I'd already been in Bangkok for several months, had done quite a lot of sightseeing, and had worked within the local economy. I also possessed the required security clearance that all mission employees needed before starting work at the embassy. I quickly got to work filling out the lengthy application form. A few hours later, I drafted a cover letter that highlighted my most relevant job-related skills and experience. I was able to hand-deliver the packet of materials, since I'd previously visited the embassy to check in and to receive my formal orientation to the mission. I could say honestly that I already knew my way around, at least to a degree.

As with all U.S. government job applications, mine went through a careful screening process involving the embassy hiring committee, whose members were asked to rate job applicants on their suitability. Several weeks later, I was called in for an interview. I tried to state clearly how Shelly and I had both made a career transition towards service-oriented work when we came to Bangkok and this job appeared to be almost entirely service-related. I emphasized my commitment to working as the go-to person for mission family members in Bangkok. The committee must have believed I was sincere, because I received the formal job offer the following week.

These kind of support positions are normally categorized as temporary and less than full time by the U.S. government. My contract was for one year. Later I gained another service position at the U.S. Foreign

Commercial Service, which was also classified as a short-term personal services contract; it didn't offer any benefits beyond the salary. This is true of so many jobs involving work that isn't labeled as mission critical, but which are significant in their impact on the community.

These jobs often involve work that is considerably more stimulating than jobs that are more closely related to mission operations. The Community Liaison Officer, or CLO, position was a consistently interesting one. This position had been created by a U.S. State Department initiative several years earlier, in response to a perceived need within the government for a clearinghouse person at each overseas post. At least one designated individual at larger posts abroad would answer the many questions that American families faced as they attempted to adapt to widely differing cross-cultural situations.

No single American possessed the expertise needed to solve all the issues that arose, so normally a CLO assistant would be hired locally to provide vital support. In my office, a very personable and culturally sensitive woman named Jeed occupied this position. Khun Jeed could be relied upon to organize her dance group in ornate Thai silks for beautiful mini-performances of the Ramayana or other classical Thai folklore on important Thai holidays such as *Songkran*, the Buddhist New Year water celebration, or *Loy Krathong*, the annual festival of lights.

The CLO job kept me busy. I was responsible for welcoming and orienting newcomers for more than twenty U.S. government agencies based in Bangkok. Because of the city's medical facilities and highly trained doctors, Bangkok served as a regional operational center for other U.S. embassies in Southeast Asia. There were regular visits by American officials from neighboring posts in Burma, Laos, and Cambodia, among others. The job brought me into regular contact with the U.S. ambassador and his wife in planning U.S. mission holiday events and reporting on the state of employee morale at the post. Considering the high visibility of the position and the direct contact I had with heads of many agencies, I was grossly underpaid. This is still the case for CLOs, who provide critical daily support to thousands of over-stretched embassy personnel and their families at U.S. missions around the world.

While it would be inappropriate for me to elaborate too much on the specifics of the job, considering the high-level security clearance it required, I can say it was a privilege to serve my country in such a far-off part of the world during an exciting era of transformations. In the early 1990s, the fall of the Berlin Wall in Europe and the massacre of student demonstrators at Tiananmen Square in Beijing were fresh in the minds of the public. The world was moving through an uncertain transition, from the Cold War era to something new and uncharted. Many admired the United States, which was acknowledged as the lone superpower in those days. It was also seen as a symbol of hope and progress. Our country's new, youthful leadership under President Bill Clinton and Vice President Al Gore was projecting a confidence and vitality that was heartening to many.

The U.S. mission in Bangkok was by far the largest single-country presence in Bangkok, with hundreds of American employees working there. The Thai government was a close partner in the level of bilateral trade, regularly scheduled joint military exercises, and promotion of democratic values. The context in which we were working consistently inspired Shelly and me to do our very best work.

The U.S. government infrastructure in the Thai capital was impressive to behold. It included a beautiful historic mansion on Wireless Road that served as the ambassador's residence and another historical building on South Sathorn Road that was used by the U.S. Information Service. There was also a separate compound for the U.S. Agency for International Development in central Bangkok and a Joint U.S.-Thailand Military (JUSMAG-Thai) compound. In short, we were the major diplomatic players and had unparalleled access to Thai decision makers.

From a "Big-C" cultural perspective, Bangkok offered many artistic and educational exhibitions and events to enjoy. The American University Alumni Association (AUA), the largest purveyor of American English and cultural programs in Thailand, was in the heart of

Bangkok, and its classes were well subscribed. AUA also had a smaller number of Thai language courses, one of which Shelly and I sampled in the hopes of studying Thai after work. Unfortunately, we found their teaching methodology, which was called the Natural Approach, impractical and passive.

This approach had been designed to expose adult students to many types of language situations that were believed to simulate the natural immersion that a child experiences when learning a language. However, it excluded the importance of conscious thought and learner motivation.[23] According to an AUA administrator on site, most language learners didn't even begin to speak in their Thai language classes until several weeks into their studies. For us, this was unimaginable, based on our Peace Corps study experience, which had already given us basic survival skills in the language in a short period of time.

When it came to "small-C" culture, those aspects of Thai behaviors and attitudes that weren't immediately apparent to foreigners, we had many to consider. For instance, we wondered why Thais were so tolerant, unlike many other peoples around the world. They were more likely than not to greet a newcomer with a warm and welcoming smile, rather than a frown. This was an important reason why the country is now flooded with visitors from all areas of the world. Many Thais have a beautiful sense of aesthetics and try to enrich their own lives and those of visitors with beautiful garlands of fragrant flowers, lovely colorful Thai silks, and exquisitely flavored Thai foods. We had a vague sense that the Buddhist concept of karma caused Thais to be sensitive to their every action, as positive or negative behaviors in the present life would affect their status in future lives.

American residents of Bangkok also experienced many surprises in their daily encounters with Thai friends and colleagues. For instance, outside of the work environment, they were prone to decide not to show up at social events, even when they promised they would attend. This reflected the Thai preference for conflict avoidance. Rather than saying no to an invitation, they preferred to respond affirmatively, bearing in mind that they would try to attend if they could, but might not if another responsibility arose. Putting on an agreeable public face was the right course of action in nearly any situation.

From a Thai perspective, a certain degree of ambiguity was preferable to a blunt refusal to a kind invitation. Of course, when Shelly and I organized after-work drinks or potluck dinners at our place, we had to guess what percentage of our Thai friends would show up and try to prepare accordingly. The Thai sense of time was baffling to many foreigners. Thais considered time to be flexible in their daily life outside of work. For sporting events, receptions, or film festivals, "Thai time" was often in effect, which meant that start times were viewed as mere suggestions. You could arrive thirty minutes late without missing anything important. Thais were accustomed to this rhythm of life when they stepped outside the Western work context. This is what anthropologist Edward T. Hall called a polychromic sense of time, and it prevails throughout Southeast Asia[24]. Thais working at the U.S. Embassy or the U.S. Peace Corps, however, had to quickly learn to adjust their perceptual frameworks to what Hall called a monochromic or task- and punctuality-oriented behavioral style. At the office, they understood the importance of operating on "Western time". They could then slip comfortably back into their relationship-oriented lifestyle at home.

Another example of how much Thai culture impacted social interchanges took place when I joined a local basketball tournament organized by the Bangkok city government. Adult basketball teams were sponsored by the Bangkok police and fire departments, a major Thai bank, and the U.S. Embassy. The contrasting styles and attitudes of the teams said a lot about cultural differences between Thais and Americans. Our basketball team was composed primarily of the U.S. Marine Corps guard contingent and some of the younger American male employees from the different U.S. agencies. Our team practiced hard for about two weeks before the tournament, running as a group in the mornings before work and then playing practice pick-up games after work whenever we could. A generous American sporting goods company in Bangkok donated the latest Air Jordan high-top basketball sneakers for all of us to use. We felt confident, to say the least. We were also excited when tournament day rolled around. When we arrived at a local high school gym that served as the venue for the event, I could tell right away that we were in for a cross-cultural lesson that might not be an easy one.

The three competing Thai teams had all brought along cheering sections dressed in the appropriate team colors: red for the Thai fire department team, green for the police department, and blue for the Thai bank. We had no color scheme, and our cheering section consisted of a handful of spouses and children we had scraped together, along with a few other supportive American and Thai colleagues from the embassy. While we probably could have considered a color scheme of red, white and blue if we'd been briefed about this cultural phenomenon at sporting events, what we ended up wearing was typical for U.S. pick-up games: tank tops or mesh athletic jerseys, polyester shorts, and of course our new black high-top shoes. We weren't exactly a dream team in those get-ups.

We also brought along our cocky American male attitudes, a sense that we could handle our smaller and presumably less experienced Thai competitors. After all, most of the Marines were twenty-five and under and in near-peak physical condition. They regularly kept fit by pumping iron and doing a wide array of calisthenics. Even I was in pretty good shape in those days, working out regularly at a new fitness club near the embassy. I wasn't exactly an old man then, either, although I was older than the Marines.

Our Thai competitors were a mix of twenty- and thirty-year old players. The tournament had been organized as a single-elimination event. There would be two first-round games in the morning and the winning teams would advance to the afternoon championship game. All but one of the teams was assured of a medal, whether it was the gold for the winner, or the silver or bronze for the teams that placed second or third. As it turned out, even the fourth-place team received a nice plaque to ensure there would be no hard feelings.

Our morning game pitted our ragtag team against the low-key Thai bankers. We were fortunate to draw them, since the players appeared to be older and less practiced than either the Thai police or fire department team. From the game's tipoff until the final bell sounded, our team outran the bankers, with our guards making a high percentage of their jump shots. We were all getting in on the high fives. We seemed to be on a lucky streak, and the game's final score wasn't even close. We were gracious winners, shaking hands with members of the opposing team afterwards, all the while smiling and assuring them they had played a great game.

We entered the championship match that afternoon against the Thai fire department team confident and ready to play a tough team. The fire fighters were the mirror opposites of the Thai bankers. They were younger, energetic, and well coached. They were also joking with each other and clearly having a grand old time. Competition for them didn't seem to be a serious matter. From the opening tip-off that our opponents controlled, it was clear we were facing a practiced foe. The loud cheers of their red-clad supporters were a kind of non-stop chant urging them on. This team's strategy was based on fast passing, slick footwork, and ball handling, and the non-stop action didn't seem to wear them down at all, even as we began to lag.

Throughout the first half, they wore us down. Our star players went cold with their shots. While I wouldn't say I saw fear in my teammates' eyes, I did detect a trace of worry that grew more pronounced as the fire fighters jumped out to a double-digit lead by halftime. As a forward, I enjoyed a height advantage over most of the Thai team, which hardly mattered since they were passing the ball so much and shooting so well. As I recall, my total point output was a paltry two baskets for the entire game.

Smaller, looser, and better coached, our Thai opponents ran away with the game in the second half. At one point, they pulled ahead by more than twenty points. This beating could easily have become a total humiliation for us, but it didn't. For that I credit the opposing team, which started easing up and allowing us to take some easy shots. They helped us pull closer. The final score had the Thai team winning by just ten points. Their supporters were ecstatic as the final bell rang.

We all felt embarrassed by our poor showing. Our egos were thoroughly crushed. Even as we were awarded silver medals during the post-game ceremony, our collective reaction was one of disappointment.

We should've learned an important cultural lesson about teamwork from this drubbing. While we were mostly acting as hot-shot NBA player wannabes, the Thais were sharing scoring opportunities among themselves. As a result, nearly all their players had shone. Our team had relied on just one or two superstar marines for most of our scoring power. Our opponents had slackened off on us when it was clear they would win, allowing us to save face. It's possible their behavior also permitted this international event to maintain the goodwill it was always meant to promote.

———

As the CLO, one of my main responsibilities was to assist in maintaining positive links between the U.S. Embassy in Bangkok and local Thai community organizations. This meant publicizing and promoting any local activities where U.S. mission officials might want to participate. As the editor of *About Bangkok*, I was forever placing advertisements related to Thai holiday celebrations, important historical events, low-cost shopping opportunities, and local and regional travel opportunities. Khun Jeed and I also tried to educate American officials on the myriad aspects of Bangkok life by launching a new column called "Thai Cultural Tips".

I really enjoyed the programs offered by the Siam Society, a Bangkok-based organization dedicated to preserving and highlighting Thailand's impressive heritage. My office organized several tours of the society and arranged for embassy attendance at scholarly presentations on topics relating to Thai textiles, ceramics, architectural styles, music, dance, and more. Supported by the Thai royal family, the society is a unique institute that exemplifies the Thais' pride in keeping alive their 800-year-old history.

It was also a pleasure to promote many special projects involving U.S. Peace Corps volunteers. These dedicated volunteers often approached the embassy for support on special drives and campaigns aimed at enhancing the quality of life of their local communities. For instance, often in the short winter season in Thailand, areas in the north and northeast of the country suffered greatly from the cold, even experiencing deaths due to exposure as temperatures dropped. Most low-income Thais didn't have enough disposable income to invest in warm clothing or blankets. It was a good thing that U.S. mission families had surplus winter gear, which they contributed in large volume.

Many poor Thai families didn't have any extra income for purchasing eyeglasses, either. Their children were frequently stunted in their capacity to learn by not being able to focus well on their written school lessons. Once again, many mission staff and family members contributed old or unused eyeglasses to Peace Corps campaigns.

Our office supported a memorable project involving a volunteer's efforts to sell artwork created by low-income children living in the giant *Klong Toey* slum of Bangkok. The volunteer, named Rob, invited the embassy to watch him teach art to street children at his work site in the slums. The slums have long received material and moral support from the world-renowned Duang Prateep Foundation. Rob introduced Khun Jeed and me to Daw Prateep Ungsongtham Hata, the inspiring Thai woman who heads the Duang Prateep Foundation. She had grown up in *Klong Toey* and through sheer willpower had managed to achieve a secondary school education. She started the foundation to support the poor of her community, and her work has been going on for decades. Her goal was to give these people a belief in themselves and hope for the future.[25]

We stopped by and observed an after-school watercolor painting class Rob was leading for a large group of young children. The kids were painting greeting cards in bright, cheerful colors that depicted themselves and domesticated animals in a light-hearted, everyday context. He explained that the cards were already being sold in tourist shops around town and through the foundation's wide network of supporters worldwide. All proceeds were funneled back into the foundation to benefit kindergarten classes, playgroups, and primary school scholarships. We were only too pleased to help in any way we could. From that point onward, we displayed the cards in our office. Many visitors bought them by the bunch, which helped us generate a significant amount of funds for the foundation.

When Shelly and I wanted to have a nice meal, there were two special restaurants we visited on many occasions for their surroundings, good service, and wonderful Thai food. Both were constructed in the traditional manner, using Thai teakwood. Their décor was guaranteed to please, with handcrafted Thai place settings, colorful seat cushions and candles, and fresh flowers at every table.

The first place was located just a few blocks from the embassy, so it was especially easy to visit right after work. The Whole Earth specialized in traditional Thai dishes, many of which were vegetarian, as well as specialties from India and other parts of Southeast Asia. Their Thai fruit smoothies were just right for cooling off after a long day of high heat and humidity in the Thai capital. My personal favorites were their yellow curries, which were consistently good, as were their *kao pad* (stir-fried rice) and *kwuyteu* (noodle plates). I can't remember a time we left without a smile on our faces. This was true of their equally special Chiang Mai location, which we visited often when we traveled in northern Thailand.

The second, which was just right for visiting with friends or Peace Corps volunteers, was called Cabbages and Condoms (C&C). This restaurant was affiliated with the Population and Community Development Center, which was best known for its family planning and HIV/AIDS outreach programs. At that time, PDA was on the front lines of educating the Thai public about behavioral changes needed to contain the alarming AIDS epidemic that had gripped the country since the late

1980s. Some of PDA's best-known events were condom balloon-blowing competitions, creating a Captain Condom mascot, and having police officers distribute condoms as part of its Cops and Rubbers Program.[26] C&C also distributed condoms in lieu of after-dinner mints at its restaurant. The restaurant's garden setting was sure to cheer up even the gloomiest visitor. On the way in and out, it was almost impossible to avoid stopping by the well-stocked gift shop, which sold beautiful native handicrafts prepared to spread the message of AIDS prevention.

Another of our favorite places for dining was our home, where we enjoyed the culinary services of Khun Teem, our talented chef and housemother. She offered us fresh tropical fruits with our breakfast and such Thai delicacies as *tom ka gai* (coconut chicken soup) and *tom yom gung* (sweet and sour shrimp soup) at dinner. Our ultimate weakness was *kao niao ma muang*, the incredible dessert made with mango and sticky rice, which is popular world-wide. Of course, this dish is guaranteed to pack the pounds on, so a routine of regular exercise is advisable if you can't help but indulge in it.

Our home truly served as our haven, especially once we installed our living room curtains and arranged the furniture just so. It was a charming two-story teakwood structure with smartly polished wooden floors covered strategically with large rice mats that served as rugs. Two honey-beige rattan sofas were adorned with overstuffed white cushions. They were perfect for sinking into for a well-deserved nap or for entertaining decent-sized groups for after-work drinks or dinner.

We had a glass top dining room table with space for twelve and attractive blue-and-white flatware, ornate silver utensils, and festive placemats for entertaining. During our time in Bangkok, we invited most of our nearest neighbors to dine with us. They were a veritable United Nations in their diversity; an older New Zealand couple, a younger Norwegian couple, and an irascible French bachelor were among our favorites.

Teem was experienced in catering to hungry volunteers. She often prepared the Thai village dishes to which they were accustomed. A specialty was her *somtam*, or fresh spicy papaya salad, which she could conjure up in no time at all. She also prepared uniquely American dishes that were often what homesick volunteers were missing. These included spaghetti and meat or vegetable sauce, fried chicken, mashed potatoes, muffins, and chocolate cake, and many other creations.

———

With so many good things to say about our Bangkok experience, there was a dark spot amid all this brightness. The transportation network in the city was severely taxed in those years, especially as the Sky Train project was finally launched and the freeway expansion effort continued unabated. The number of cars on the roads far exceeded what they had been built to sustain. Daily commuting was a wrenching ordeal that involved making a critical decision about which route might contain slightly fewer cars than others.

The solution to the traffic mess for most American officials was to leave as early as possible in the morning for work, just to survive the drive with minimum stress. Many arrived at work as early as 6:30 am. Returning home by 3:30 or four o'clock in the afternoon might—or might not—save you from the normal afternoon gridlock, depending on the season. During the rainy season, the huge traffic jam that consumed the city might last all day long.

The traffic in Bangkok proceeded on the left, in the British style. That meant cars were right-wheel. For the first few weeks of driving there, Shelly and I had to remind ourselves regularly to bear left, as we unconsciously drifted right when we weren't focused on our driving. In any case, the traffic speed never got much faster than thirty kilometers per hour, except on weekends, so there was little chance of a serious accident. Still, we did have the occasional shock of seeing another vehicle heading straight at us as we darted quickly from the right-hand lane. Shelly was exceedingly fortunate in that we lived only a few miles away from her office on Ratchawithi road. Her morning drive was only ten or fifteen minutes.

After we'd purchased our own car, my normal commute took me from our home in the northwest section of Bangkok across to the U.S. Embassy in the southeast section. The drive was repeated in the opposite direction on the way home. Assuming I got started before seven o'clock in the morning, this would normally involve a forty-five-to-sixty-minute drive. The fastest route took me through the heart of the city, along Ratchawithi road eastward to Rama V road southward, then along Sri Ayutthaya road, which skirted the Royal Palace, eastward to Rama VI road southward. This would take me to Phetburi road eastward and through the heavily congested public market district. Finally, a right turn would take me across Rama I road and finally down Wireless Road, where the embassy was located. This route is firmly etched in my memory more than two decades later, precisely because there were so many trial-and-error attempts before I got it right.

The main issue was deciphering the right way to get to work in the years before Google maps and GPS. It meant I invariably got lost or turned around before I finally understood what worked. When accidents occurred along my preferred route, I needed to improvise some sort of alternative way. This would all add to the time required to reach the office or home. While I professed to work an early schedule, this was often modified if I arrived as late as ten o'clock. In those cases, my departure time from work would have to be pushed back to six o'clock or even later.

The traffic situation could have been a truly wretched one for all concerned, but again the Thais proved to be surprising serene amid the chaos. The use of horns and obnoxious behaviors, including road rage, that occur in similar gridlock situations in the West were relatively rare on the packed roads of Bangkok. And certain areas of the city were interesting to look at when stopped, especially in the older sections. So, if I had to sit in traffic for extended periods of time, I had the pleasure of studying unusual architecture. Certain industrious vendors, street performers, and beggars lingered near the busiest intersections, too, so there was normally some entertainment and local snacks to enjoy.

Many of the principal roads in Bangkok were named after the country's most esteemed monarchs. Rama I Road, for instance, was named
after the founder of the current Chakri dynasty King Phra Phutthayotfa
Chulalok[27], who designated Rattanakosin, later called Bangkok, as the
capital city in 1782. This key byway bisected the center of town, from
touristy Sukhumvit road through the Siam Center shopping district to
the historic part of Bangkok. Rama IV Road, named after revered King
Mongut, who spent many of his adult years as a Buddhist monk, intersected an important commercial section farther south of the city
center. Rama V Road, named after King Chulalongkorn of *The King and
I* fame, who was arguably the most Westernized of Thailand's monarchs,
divided the Royal Dusit Palace from the royal residence in the Dusit
neighborhood of Bangkok. This direct link between the roaring street
traffic of modern Bangkok and the historic and revered royal family
proved to be one of many ironies in daily life.

By late 1995, our time in Thailand was coming to an end. As with any
move from a place we'd come to love, we were torn by the endless tasks
that needed doing in too little time, while preserving a cheerful face
for our many Thai and American Peace Corps and embassy friends. We
scrambled to find new employment for Khun Teem, finally locating an
incoming American military couple who were impressed by her English
and cooking skills. They also had space in their high-rise apartment for
Teem's husband and daughter. Teem's ties to the Peace Corps came to
an end at that time, as did her village style of living in our compound.
We hoped that by then she was ready to live in the more modern style
of wealthier Bangkok residents.

Our work situation was unusual at that point. Normally, most U.S.
Peace Corps staff members would have had an opportunity to bid on another overseas tour at the successful conclusion of their first contract.
Since Shelly had worked hard and well in Thailand, we were expecting
to work and live in another developing country, although not necessarily

in Asia. Unfortunately, this wasn't a typical time for U.S. government employees. The new Republican majority in Congress was implementing what it called the "Contract with America," which swept the party to power in the 1994 elections. The contract basically stated that the U.S. government was too big and spent too much, and that Congress and unelected bureaucrats had become so entrenched as to be unresponsive to the public they were supposed to serve. The GOP contract was meant to restore accountability to government.[28] Whether that occurred or not, from the start of the 104th Congress in January 1995, the legislative branch had been in constant conflict with then President Clinton about federal spending and the direction of government.

There were two shutdowns of the federal government in quick succession at the very time we were winding down our work in Bangkok. They created great uncertainty among employees like us in the international development sector. The first shutdown lasted six days in mid-November 1995, the second one even longer, from mid-December 1995 to early January 1996.[29] I was one of many furloughed government contractors being told to quit. It was a jarring bit of news to receive while living overseas. Many of us were told to pack up and move back to the U.S. as soon as possible.

The timing coincided with the end of my first year working as a personal service contractor for the U.S. Foreign Commercial Service, a job I'd taken directly after serving my one year as the CLO. This furlough wasn't as traumatic as it might have been, as Shelly's contract with the U.S. Peace Corps was also scheduled to end soon. We had been preparing to leave Thailand anyway. Those who expected to continue working on their U.S. government project, who weren't considered to be essential employees in the eyes of the U.S. government, felt the rug pulled out from under them. They were left without a paycheck for several months. U.S. consular operations were also shuttered for all but emergency cases, leaving many travelers who were awaiting new or renewed passports without recourse. Such actions had a huge and negative impact on public perceptions of the U.S. government around the world.

Our departure from Bangkok and from Asia after more than seven eventful years coincided with this unprecedented U.S. government shutdown. Starting that November, all decisions regarding future hiring by any U.S. government agency had been put on hold for an indefinite period. It became increasingly clear to us that we'd most likely have to abandon our plans for additional U.S. government-sponsored development work.

Soon after our arrival back to the States, we took refuge for several months in the southern California desert home of our good friend Bill Gay, who had been active in the cross-cultural training groups we'd joined in Tokyo. He'd been offered a teaching position in Japan for a semester and needed house sitters to keep an eye on things back home. We were only too glad to step in. We both badly needed quiet time for charting a new course and stepping away from the non-stop activity of our Bangkok tour. We ended up staying in sunny southern California while we looked for a new challenge in a different geographical region. This down time was a blessing. We could refresh and refocus, something everyone should do during major life transitions.

3: Bucharest, Romania

Cine are carte are parte!—A Romanian Proverb
(He who has a book has power!)

Bucharest was a dramatic change after our Asia sojourn. It became, for us, an acquired taste. The city, and indeed all of Romania, had been long shrouded in secrecy until the dark decades of Soviet domination finally came to a screeching halt in 1989. The city still gave off an air of mystery when we arrived there in the mid-1990s. Both Shelly and I felt we were learning about the city and Romanian culture from the ground up during our two years there.

By the time we'd departed Bangkok, we were looking for new opportunities in a different region of the world. Like many in those years, we were aware of the important geo-political transitions that were taking place in Central and Eastern Europe after the fall of the Berlin Wall. Previously Communist states were struggling to transition to democratically-run, or at least democratic-seeming, societies. The fall of the Berlin Wall a few years earlier had unleashed a domino effect that had taken down so many authoritarian regimes, starting with East Germany and continuing to the former Soviet Union.

We were amazed by the speed of the social and political changes that were taking place and hoped they'd continue to spread democratic values and reforms even farther afield. It seemed quite plausible then that even the unpredictable Yeltsin regime in Moscow might usher in a more open society with a market economy in Russia. Some harbored a faint hope that China's highly centralized government might move in the same reformist direction. Despite the U.S. government shutdowns that were occurring, those years were characterized by high hopes and optimistic projections for our rapidly globalizing world.

Many Americans were basking in the newfound international admiration and respect for American democratic values that had won the Cold War. The world, it seemed, was looking to the U.S. for enlightened leadership and a new direction. Shelly and I hoped to assist our country's efforts in any way we could. Fortunately, several successful American entrepreneurs had once hailed from Central or Eastern Europe and some were taking up the challenge of helping to rebuild their native region. One such individual was the Hungarian-American business magnate George Soros, who founded the Soros Foundation, later renamed the Open Society Institute (OSI). Its mission was to build vibrant and tolerant democracies whose governments are accountable and open to the participation of all people.[30]

We supported Soros's philosophy wholeheartedly. We were ready to explore the fast-changing countries of Eastern Europe, and we soon learned that the foundation had launched a large-scale reform effort in former Communist states aimed at restructuring the curricula and teaching methods at leading universities. Its overarching goal was to direct them toward successful Western-style models. Since we had previously taught at the university level in Asia, Shelly at the University of Maryland near Tokyo and me at Mahidol University near Bangkok, we thought that we should enlist in such an inspiring program.

We contacted project managers specializing in educational reform at the Soros Foundation by email, a new and fast developing mode of communication at the time. Their reform project was called the Civic Education Project, or CEP. The representative explained what we would require in our application packets. It was clear they were targeting certain fields for their initiative, including business, management, and law. When word came a few weeks later that we'd both been selected as visiting fellows, we were very excited. We learned our compensation would consist of a monthly stipend supplemented by our local teaching salaries and that free housing would be provided. We'd be responsible for our food, local transport, and utility costs.

We had no idea where we would be placed. When asked on the CEP application form to select three preferred choices, we'd opted for Hungary, Romania, and Albania, in that order. CEP had tried to locate two teaching slots for us that would be close to each other in one of these preferred places. What we received was an offer for two faculty positions at the Academy of Economic Studies (ASE) in Bucharest, Romania. After a short hesitation, we accepted.

We knew very little about Romania. Whatever impressions we'd formed were inextricably linked to the country's ruthless former dictator, Nicolae Ceauşescu, and the violent uprising that led to his execution in 1989. Beyond that, we were intrigued by Bram Stoker's tale of Count Dracula, another horribly charismatic Romanian leader. His literary legend was based on the actual life of Vlad the Impaler, who had lived in Transylvania in the 17th century. His life had been filled with gruesome cruelty. Beyond that, like most other Americans, we were only familiar with the country's stellar gymnasts, such as Nadia Comaneci, who'd performed so superbly in the Olympics during the 1970's, exhibiting a grace and precision that had approached perfection.

Shelly also had an important emotional link to the Balkans. The daughter of a U.S. development official, she'd spent her early childhood in Greece when her father worked there. Shelly had loved the simpler, unspoiled lifestyle of Greece and often spoke wistfully about it. We'd traveled to Greece a few times and had found it captivating. We hoped that our teaching placements in the nearby Balkans would allow us to travel to Greece, Turkey, Cyprus, and other parts of the Eastern Mediterranean, to get to know them.

The diversity and dynamism of the Balkans grabbed our attention and our imaginations, even though the entire region was still reeling under the effects of the violent breakup of the former Yugoslavia, which had led to constant fighting and genocidal acts in the emerging State of Bosnia-Herzegovina. We could predict that our upcoming experience in Bucharest was likely to be very different from our journeys to Tokyo and Bangkok. This new adventure would likely involve learning new ways to cope with daily hardships and fast-changing lifestyles.

———•———

Before departing for Romania, we attended several days of pre-departure orientation provided by CEP at Yale University in late summer. We received a lot of "Big-C" cultural information about Romania's strategic location at a major crossroads in Eastern Europe, its diverse ethnic mix, and its long, bittersweet history. Over the centuries, the country had managed to absorb the enlightenment of the West and the mysticism of the East. Not surprisingly, it has encountered more than its share of foreign invaders, most of whom ruled the territories of Romania with an iron fist.

Romania's huge Transylvania region in the northwestern part of the country was long part of the Austro-Hungarian Empire and even to this day has remained culturally and commercially close to its Hungarian neighbors. Much of the rest of Romania, including the regions of Walachia and Moldavia, was under Turkish domination for more than five hundred years, until the end of the 19th century. Those two regions struggled to create a unified country. What became modern Romania—including Transylvania—reunited for a brief period as a sovereign nation following World War I. Unfortunately, after just two decades of unity, the country was once again torn asunder by German occupiers. The latter months of World War II brought different foreign occupiers; Soviet troops installed a pro-Communist regime in the country. From that point onward, Soviet hegemony clamped a lid on Romania that wouldn't be released for more than four decades.

With so many centuries of upheaval in the region's history, the Romanian language and culture are incredibly rich and multi-layered. Romanian is a hybrid language that owes its roots to the Latin of classical Rome, but also includes words of Turkish, Greek and Slavic origin. The language is full of unique and puzzling aspects that inspire and animate Romanian. While we were living in Bucharest, our local friends often expressed the view that they were able to understand Italian speakers with relative ease. Native Italians, they assured us, had less success in comprehending modern Romanian.

The country is a marvel to behold. It still has many majestic castles, some surviving medieval towns, and all kinds of wildlife that long ago disappeared from Western Europe.[31] It's part of a wide swath of geography including Ukraine and Moldova that was still largely undiscovered in the Eastern bloc, even up to the 1990s. We were soon to discover how different Romania was from the rest of Europe. Still, the young revolutionaries that had toppled the decadent old Ceaușescu regime were bound and determined to push the country ahead towards the Western model of development and eventual European Union membership.

At our orientation at Yale University, we first met our cohort of six other American teaching fellows who had been assigned to Romania. Three others were placed in Bucharest for the year, two had been assigned to Cluj-Napoca in Transylvania, and one would be stationed in Timisoara, near the Serbian border. We were a diverse group in the sense that our academic interests spanned business, law, and literature. At the same time, we all seemed to possess international travel experiences and were old enough to cope with the upcoming rigors we expected to face in the country.

During informal discussions, our orientation coordinators warned us that academic cultures in Eastern Europe were stodgy and hidebound and that we Americans would pose a threat to the interests of some long-term stakeholders. They also made it clear that the new government in Bucharest, along with the progressive youth movements that had led both peaceful and violent uprisings, were strongly in favor of a radical change in educational practices. We would be placed at local universities to serve as symbols of the dramatic change that so many were yearning for, but also feared, due to the negative associations of earlier foreign misrule. They cautioned us to be prepared to explain ourselves and to defend our reasons for introducing new ideas, especially with more senior university administrators and faculty.

At the end of CEP's orientation, we were again facing the imminent prospect of an overseas move. As on earlier occasions, we had just a short time to pack our household effects and to sell, give away, or store the rest. We had rented a large storage unit in Southern California after moving back from Bangkok, so we could add whatever items we couldn't take. Rested, young, and energetic, we decided to do a self-move with the help of a large U-Haul van and a few local friends. Teaching volunteers in Bucharest had only a small budget for shipping anything beyond what we could carry ourselves. We labeled these as intended for educational purposes and shipped them as airfreight.

By this time, we'd mastered the art of packing. We protected the few nice antiques we'd acquired in Asia in tightly sealed bubble-wrap plastic to keep out the dust in our storage unit. We stored our light cotton clothing and textiles, which wouldn't adapt well to the Romanian winters, in mothballs, to ward off moths and other pesky invaders. We placed them in plastic and then in heavy cardboard boxes that were stacked carefully along one wall in our unit. The electronic items and other household appliances we'd acquired were mostly small—a toaster oven, television monitor, and boom box—since we had been living in rental housing for so long. These didn't take up much space.

Our focus, as usual, was on the many boxes of textbooks, training materials, novels, travel brochures, and photo albums we'd accumulated in our years of wandering. As the World Wide Web was just emerging, we had grown accustomed to hoarding and hauling many printed items that either had special significance to us or might one day be needed. Moving these had been a labor of love, but we were growing weary at the thought of hauling them once again. Most of these would remain in storage, since we lacked the means to send them all.

We managed to fill two large duffle bags of teaching supplies and quality-of-life niceties for Romania. Each bag measured six feet long by three feet wide and weighed much more than the normal allotment of

fifty pounds per bag. We delivered these to Delta Airline's cargo shipment facility at Los Angeles International Airport (LAX) several hours
before our scheduled flight. They would be forwarded on to Bucharest
and they managed to arrive there before we did.

Delta was the main American carrier from the U.S. to Eastern
Europe. Their customs and shipping requirements were daunting and
required several hours to ensure that the inventory list, official shipping bill, and destination contact information were verified and in order.
The local contact for CEP in Bucharest, a young woman named Andrea,
had told us we could use her name and local office address for our shipments, which seemed reassuring at the time.

For our trip to Bucharest, we arranged an all–Delta routing that
would take us from LAX to New York's Kennedy Airport, with onward connections to Paris's Charles de Gaulle Airport and Bucharest's
Otopeni International Airport. Flight time was about fifteen hours in
sardine-can style economy class seating. With the overnight stopover
in New York and a lengthy transit period in Paris, our journey seemed
to take forever, especially since we always seemed to be traveling in the
dark. As on earlier overseas trips, we had a restless kitty in tow under
the seat, our furry Persian named Fujiko that we'd adopted in Japan.
Our intrepid Himalayan cat, which had enlivened our flights to Tokyo
and Bangkok, had gone missing in Bangkok and was never found, to
our profound dismay.

———•———

We arrived in Bucharest, or *Bucuresti* as the locals call it, in late morning on a gray summer's day. It was a good thing that a CEP driver was
there to meet us at the airport and assist with the local customs officials,
since we spoke no Romanian at all. Bucharest was still a rather insular
place, just a handful of years removed from the stifling Communist era,
so not many travel industry personnel spoke English. Due to historic
links between Romania and France, though, quite a few officials spoke

French, and there were some signs in French at places where tourists gathered.

Our brains were as cloudy as that day was turning out to be. Our jetlag was as deep as it had ever been after any overseas flight. We were in no mood to process a lot of new logistical or cultural challenges, so we rejoiced when the Romanian airport inspector simply glanced for a moment at our cat's health and vaccination certificates and then waved us through. We'd lucked out just as we had in Tokyo. We hurried to the bulk shipment area across the arrivals terminal to collect our duffle bags and were forced to wait for over an hour.

When our parcels finally showed up, we discovered that one had been ripped open and pilfered, most likely at the destination point, although we couldn't prove it. Our losses included a power adapter and a clock radio. We didn't hang around to complain, as we were too tired. We signed the release forms for our shipments and exited the airport. Our strongest wish at that moment was to drag ourselves and our bedraggled kitty as quickly as possible to any type of bed.

Our drive into the city was mercifully brief in comparison to many airport transfers. It was by now Sunday afternoon in Bucharest and motor vehicle traffic was light. A glimpse of the Sofitel Airport Hotel reinforced our initial impression that the French were well established in Romania. We passed heavy forest cover on the outskirts of the city and traveled down some nice boulevards as we headed towards the city center.

Driving through one massive plaza surrounded by beautiful colonial-era buildings and other large modern buildings in various stages of construction, our driver informed us that we were at *Piata Victoriei*, or Victory Square, the heart of Bucharest. This is where the Romanian Palace, the seat of government, was located. Our destination was nearby, on Titulescu Boulevard, one of the spokes veering off from the wheel of the huge Victory Square. This gave us hope that we'd be living near a cosmopolitan part of the city, which proved to be the case. We finally reached our new home a few minutes later and prepared to decamp.

We were on our last legs when we first saw the drab, cement-block building that would serve as our home for the next year. We were too tired to notice many of the exterior details, beyond its hulking ten floors and the solid-looking entrance that was straight ahead of us as we unloaded suitcases, two large duffle bags, and the kitty carrier. Our driver helped move all our stuff from the curb up to our third-floor apartment. Unfortunately, we didn't have any Romanian *lei*, the local currency, to tip him, so I slipped him a ten-dollar bill instead and sent him on his way. We saw few people on the street or in our building. It was a very sleepy Sunday in our new neighborhood, which suited us fine.

When we opened the door to our apartment, our first impression was that the place hadn't been lived in for some time. The dim lighting and musty smell took some adjustment, even in broad daylight. An initial scan of the unit indicated a long and narrow railroad-car layout. The master bedroom was situated to the left off the main hallway and a small guest room to the right. As we proceeded in, we saw a small square kitchen to the left and a rectangular combination living and dining area at the end of the railcar. A door at the far-left corner led onto a long, narrow balcony that overlooked the boulevard below. We dropped our many belongings in the living area and began a cursory inspection of the apartment.

Our eyes turned towards the curtains. It was immediately clear that they'd been shut tight for a long time, as the tassels were tied tightly around them. Drawing them provided some sunlight, but only a little. Next, we discovered that the living room furniture was covered in white sheets. Removing the sheets revealed a sofa and two chairs of the heavy, brocaded sort popular in Europe in the early 20th century. Not surprisingly, these pieces were heavily worn and fading to gray. There was a dark wood elongated coffee table to complement them, with a Romanian style red, white, and black-checked runner on top. The carpet was scarlet, with faux royal motifs to liven the look.

The walls were a sooty color which indicated that smokers had long lived on the premises. We opened the windows as wide as they would go to start airing the place. We stood outside on our new balcony, which had a good view of Titulescu Boulevard. A yellow streetcar sped by with a clack-clack sound. Our street, it turned out, was on a main line for the tram system that crisscrossed Bucharest. That would turn out to be a convenient way for getting to our university jobs. We looked around the balcony and wondered if a lounger or two deck chairs might fit in. Of course, we were fated never to find such items in Bucharest, so we ended up using our balcony primarily for storage of bulk items. We even preserved fruits and vegetables there during the winter.

A few steps back inside took us to our new kitchen, or rather our retro kitchen. The appliances seemed like those our parents might have used in their early married life decades earlier. The gas stove was attached to a very small oven unit that provided basic space for cooking a simple meal at home. The boxy refrigerator, which lacked a freezer unit, provided only a modicum of storage space for keeping food and beverages cool.

We were quickly learning that the Communist era of consumer privation had carried over into the new age of Western-style aspirations in Romania. The low quality of life hadn't changed much from the grim old days for ordinary Romanians. Many years would pass before some, but not most, Bucharest residents could upgrade to the modern appliances that Westerners took for granted.

Our final stop on this walk-through was the master bedroom, where we found a double bed covered by a warm-looking handmade quilt of red and white, even though it was summer. We wouldn't need it for several more weeks. We stripped it off the bed and put it away in a dark wood cupboard. Opening the side table drawers next to the bed, we discovered a full array of medical supplies, such as bandages, scissors, rubbing alcohol, and prescription drugs, indicating that the previous resident had likely been infirm and possibly dying in this very bed. A glance in the closet confirmed our suspicions. Nobody had removed the poor lady's garments after she'd passed on.

Andrea, CEP's project manager for Romania, later confirmed to us that an elderly woman who had been living with her husband in our apartment for decades had indeed died there a few months earlier. Her spouse had then fled Bucharest and moved in with relatives in the country. He'd never had the heart to come back and empty the place out, but he was willing to rent it to short-term boarders, to bring in some much-needed income. Life in the new, capitalistic era was particularly hard on the Romanian elderly, who were in no way ready for economic competition. Andrea explained that CEP had encountered great difficulties in procuring short-term lodgings in housing-scarce Bucharest. This required certain compromises on everyone's part for anyone needing housing near the city center.

On our first day in the country, we cringed at the thought of the poor woman who had inhabited our bed. In truth, we had no alternative but to clear away her medicines and supplies, strip the bed, change the sheets, and collapse on it for about twelve hours of overdue sleep. The next morning, the start of our first complete day in Bucharest, we began making a list of ways in which we could make our new place cleaner, more cheerful, and more comfortable.

Scrubbing and painting the walls a bright white was at the very top of our list. We also wanted to find some lighter-colored slipcovers to disguise our faded furniture. In addition, we needed to find a cooler that we could fill with ice and use as a type of freezer for perishable food items. It would take several weeks to complete all of this, since our arrival schedule included a week-long CEP in-country orientation starting right away. That, in turn, was followed by introductions and meetings with our new deans, teaching colleagues, and the staffs at our respective universities.

———•———

The CEP in-country orientation took place at the Open Society Institute (OSI) Romania office. OSI was the local branch of the Soros Foundation and was located right on Victory Square, not far from our assigned teaching spots at ASE. To get to OSI, we boarded a streetcar in front of our apartment building on Titulescu Boulevard and rode directly to

Victory Square. On our first working day, we managed to find a nearby exchange window for converting our U.S. dollars into Romanian *lei* at the going black market rate. What moneylenders were willing to trade for always differed greatly from the official government exchange rate. Our initial haul of 7,000 lei to the dollar seemed like a veritable fortune. We didn't yet know that streetcar drivers didn't accept cash. They expected riders to have purchased a monthly or daily card that would be inserted into a validation box near the entrance as proof of payment.

As we boarded our packed tram, we watched others form a line to validate their cards. Having no card ourselves, we felt panicky for a moment, but also noticed that several younger riders were simply sitting down without validating anything. We copied them, as we didn't want to be late for our first day's activities. We hoped that their behavior indicated that students or teachers or perhaps both might be exempt from paying streetcar fares. Deep down, though, we knew that there must have been a different explanation.

It turned out the Bucharest tram operated on an honor code system. Riders were expected to purchase fare cards and validate them each time they boarded. In practice, many cash-strapped students avoided the required last step whenever their funds were in short supply. Naturally, there were a few days each month when the transit police would randomly board the trams and check that all riders had punched their tickets at the machines. Those who had not faced the shame of public reprimands and a steep penalty to pay. Those who couldn't afford it were evicted from the tram as a kind of public shaming.

We were lucky that first day that the tram monitors didn't hop on board. We'd escaped a humiliating encounter without even knowing it. At our orientation, when we'd asked about local tram-riding practices, we'd learned that imitating the locals might lead us to questionable behaviors. We were encouraged to follow all local rules. This was our first cross-cultural lesson in Bucharest. There would be many more to come.

The OSI staff directed us to the training room for our official welcoming and orientation. We reconnected with our small American cohort of CEP program colleagues and met Andrea and her assistant in person, as well as several Romanian teaching colleagues who had already completed their Soros-funded studies abroad and were newly assigned to local universities. One of these Romanian colleagues, Liliana, had studied law in London and was preparing to teach at the University of Bucharest, with the additional aim of organizing judicial reform in the country. Another colleague, Radu, was teaching economics at ASE, but hadn't yet been abroad. He was hoping to pursue post-graduate studies in international management at IESE Business School in Barcelona, one of Europe's leading universities. At that time, it seemed like the sky was the limit for young and idealistic Romanians hoping to point their country in a new direction once they'd established the appropriate links with Soros funders.

We received a great overview of OSI activities in Romania to kick off our training. Romania was undergoing a major sociopolitical transition, so there were many areas where OSI could focus, and OSI seemed to have a foothold in many of them. We heard about their efforts to promote a free press, restore public trust in the political parties, foster an emerging non-profit sector, lobby for women's rights, clean up the environment, raise the public's consciousness of educational inequalities, and a multitude of other initiatives.

We fellows understood our role as change agents in promoting an unprecedented mega-shift in the country's public life, at least among the young people who would be attending our classes and workshops. Whether or not this would lead to changes at the deeper societal level impacting basic values and attitudes was still unknown to us. We divided into informal groups, to share our proposed university curricula and describe what teaching methods we planned to use. Shelly and I were both slated to teach international management courses at ASE that year. We had been placed on two different campuses that were located on opposite sides of Plaza Romana, the educational heart of Bucharest. I was also assigned to teach a course entitled Economic Case Studies, which would cover different models of economic development.

Undergraduate students who chose to immerse themselves in a foreign language environment were enrolled on my campus. They had the option of English, French, or German for their course of study. These students needed a high level of competence in the language they selected. Shelly's campus was somewhat different, more integrated into the mainstream Romanian higher education system. She'd be teaching students who were taking business-related courses, mostly in Romanian, with just a few of their courses offered in English. For that reason, their linguistic skills in English were more varied. Many were advanced level, but a fair number of students were at the intermediate level, too. Typically, a Romania-based professor at either campus conducted two formal lectures per week for each course, as well as one informal seminar meant to provide an opportunity for discussing the main points in a more collegial and participatory context. Classes turned out to be large, ranging from fifty students to one hundred or more.

In structure and learner goals, the classes we'd teach mirrored the ones I'd studied in back in Montpellier, France two decades earlier. Again, the influence of French culture on Romania's was strikingly evident. This also demonstrated that certain, if not most, European societies expected a formal professor-to-student relationship that hinged on the professor's key role as a one-way provider of his accumulated knowledge. Before long, we'd be expected to perform this role in our own classrooms. However, most of us had opted to move in a radical new direction that would motivate many of our students and colleagues while perplexing others.

Many of the ideas and suggestions we were sharing would be put into practice in a matter of weeks, at the start of the fall semester. In the meantime, we began learning survival skills for daily living in Bucharest. We started by going shopping for groceries and other household items at local shops. It wasn't long before we realized they wouldn't meet our basic food needs. Breads were made with refined white flour and vegetables were limited to whatever was in season. It looked as if we'd have to cope with a very restricted diet. Fortunately, a new Greek-run food emporium opened on Victory Square that fall and offered nearly anything we could want, although at highly inflated prices that most locals couldn't afford.

We also dined at several local restaurants with our new Romanian and international teaching colleagues, trying Romanian specialties: *ciorba* (a hearty soup), *sarmales* (stuffed cabbage rolls), and white wines from the Danube River delta. We also sought vegetarian dining options, which, not surprisingly, were quite scarce. We were excited to learn that a Pizza Hut had recently opened near Plaza Romana; it offered a salad bar–something otherwise unknown in Romania. We ate more salads and cheese pizzas than we ever had or have since.

Together with our new CEP colleague Yasmin, an Indian lady who had completed her graduate degree in the U.S., we had time to do some sightseeing in Bucharest while our workloads were still light. We walked the length of Boulevard Victoriei and beyond. One of our favorite places to visit was the beautiful Herastrau Park, which seemed to transport us beyond the bounds of the city with its rustic atmosphere, its lush tree-lined trails, and its tranquil lake. At the other end of Bucharest, we discovered the equally enchanting Cismigiu Park, which we reached via subway and a short hike.

From our first subway ride onward, we had mixed reactions to the conditions we found there. While the subway system was in good condition and the fares weren't bad, there always seemed to be legions of street people asking for handouts at the entrances. Among these were elderly pensioners who had lost most or all their life savings during the transition period from Communism to democracy, when the Romanian lei had been devalued several times. Gangs of bedraggled street kids also roamed the platforms, dressed in little more than rags and we often saw them sniffing glue. As educators, we were dismayed, knowing they should have been in school, or at least home with their families.

In our search for spiritual support, Shelly and I began attending religious services at *Sacre Coeur* Catholic Church, which, despite its French affiliation, offered a mass in English once a week. The church parishioners, many of whom hailed from the diplomatic enclave and from older, established neighborhoods, constituted an important community for us throughout our stay in Bucharest. We enjoyed the lively English language service each Sunday morning, which featured raucous singing and dancing. A few charismatic Nigerians and Filipinos had taken the lead in making worship there a joyful experience. Of course, this type of religious activity was the antithesis of the more somber Romanian Orthodox Church services.

Gradually we became acquainted with the parish priest, whom every one called Pere. It was he who conducted the English service. We also had the pleasure of meeting several nuns who had been assigned to do social work in Bucharest. Two of them, Sisters Maeve and Margaret, were amazingly unflappable and cheerful women with whom we shared many a chuckle. They had been working with the local orphanages in Bucharest for quite some time, caring for AIDS orphans. Local health care workers had unwittingly infected the children with the HIV virus, believing that by injecting blood into the children's bodies, they were providing a nutritional supplement. The Romanian officials hadn't yet recognized or accepted the dangers of AIDS, so dirty needles were used and reused. Public health estimates indicated that up to 10,000 children contracted HIV in the country's orphanages[32].

Pere's causes included a food bank and soup kitchen for the poor, as well as caring for young male migrant workers, primarily from South Sudan, who had fled their country to escape civil war and famine. The first major exodus from South Sudan occurred in the mid-1990s; eventually the numbers of displaced Sudanese grew to nearly four million people before the country was eventually recognized as the State of South Sudan.[33] Granted, Romania wasn't exactly a huge receiving country for desperate migrants in those days, being as poor as it was, but many did travel from Africa to Europe via Turkey. From Turkey, they headed northwest towards Western Europe, stopping at least for a while in Romania. Quite a number of these migrants turned up at *Sacre Coeur* after making their perilous journeys with nothing but the clothes on their backs and nowhere else to go. When we joined the church that September, we didn't realize it would be such a center for compassionate outreach to the marginalized populations of Bucharest. We simply appreciated the warm welcome we received as strangers there. We were grateful to worship there for an hour or two each week.

While preparing for our upcoming university classes, Shelly and I reassured ourselves that our dramatically new teaching methodologies were long overdue if our students were to survive and prosper one day in the reform-oriented, pro-European Union nation that Romania was trying to become. We understood that many of Romania's future leaders would want to pursue graduate education in the West, just as our Romanian teaching colleague, Liliana, had done. To gain the credentials that would set them up to work successfully in international business or government, they would need to know how to operate in a Western-style work environment. In addition, they would need to gain access to Soros funds or other E.U. scholarship monies coming available at that time, since the costs of study abroad were prohibitive for most Romanians.

Beyond our course content, we also focused on tasks that we had required students in other undergraduate programs to fulfill. For example, both Shelly and I felt that our Romanian students should be able to make an effective oral presentation to an audience. They should also learn how to write a five-page report on an important management issue and analyze a business case study as part of a project team. The teams would be presenting their recommendations in oral and written form to the class. While our class assignments might have seemed straightforward to a Western educator, in fact they challenged the entrenched traditions of Romanian university education. Romanian classes were rigidly teacher-centered, based on standardized syllabi across disciplines. Professors typically evaluated students on their final oral and written examination performance.

We were intending to customize our syllabi according to what we felt were the most critical learning objectives for our students, with their evaluations based on these, not some externally imposed standards.

Without knowing it at the time, we were using an approach that emphasized formative assessment of student learning as much or more than
summative assessment. Formative assessment meant we would help
students identify their strengths and weaknesses and target areas that
needed improvement during the learning process. The system then at
work in Romania was summative in nature, defined as evaluating student learning at the end of an instructional unit and comparing it to an
established benchmark.[34]

Several days before classes began, Shelly and I accompanied Andrea
to meet our two ASE deans. Mine was an amiable French-speaking
man. Shelly's was more serious, and his manner seemed traditionally
Romanian. He did possess good English-speaking skills, however. In
both meetings, it took Andrea's firm, persuasive efforts, linked with our
personal charm, to reassure each dean that our teaching methods, while
unorthodox from the Romanian perspective, would achieve positive
results for their students. We assured each dean that we would open
their minds to a completely different way of learning. Our new methods
were also meant to provide our students with useful late 20th-century
work skills. We understood that we ran the risk of alienating those
students who were already vested in the traditional ways of learning
in Romania or who were not really looking internationally for their inspiration and life advantages. But they numbered less than the majority
in our classrooms.

The first day of classes finally arrived. Shelly and I dressed for success in our dark tailored suits, ready to face an exciting new challenge,
but unsure of what awaited us. This moment represented a key point
during a cross-cultural academic exchange program of this type. You,
the participant, are placed in a position to face new, often unpredictable, circumstances that require your accumulated experience, quick
wit, and intercultural sensitivity to manage. Such was the case for me
as I walked to the front of the spacious amphitheater where my first
class was held, placed my briefcase on the desk, stood at the podium,
and faced sixty or so undergraduate students.

I perceived right away that establishing order would be harder than

I had expected. The students continued to chat amiably among themselves as I tried to introduce myself. Meanwhile, many students on my roster had yet to arrive. My earlier experiences teaching in Thailand and Japan had spoiled me, since students showed great deference to their professors. In Bucharest, students felt it was their right to behave in any way they wished, at least when it came to following instructions and paying full attention in class. It would be up to me to grab and hold their attention as best I could if I was going to build a workable learning environment.

I was able to draw upon the methods I'd used while teaching after-hours English classes in Japan years earlier. The secret came down to knowing how to warm up a restless audience. At that moment, I turned and drew a giant map of the United States on the blackboard behind the podium. I sketched a few American landmarks on it, such as the Rocky Mountains, Disney World, and the Statue of Liberty. And then I started over, introducing myself to my class. I explained that these were a few of my favorite places in my country and asked them to think of a few of their favorite places or things in Romania. After offering a few moments for reflecting, I went row by row and asked each student to stand up and to give a brief self-introduction.

This activity took them completely by surprise. I was pleased by the excitement generated by sharing personal information. I was learning the most from this activity. My students were describing with obvious pride their rugged Carpathian Mountains, their beautiful blue monasteries in Moldavia, the popular ski resorts of Sinaia, such notable castles as Bran and Peles, and the pristine nature reserves nearby in the Danube Delta. They spoke of Bucharest's picturesque parks, which Shelly and I had been enjoying, but also of their opulent Opera House, their intriguing National Village Museum, and their famous native son, the poet Mihai Eminescu. What a wonderful way to learn about Romanian culture!

I was immensely fortunate to receive such an impressive overview of Romania's treasures from the many enthusiastic students in my International Management class. They seemed pleased to have a professor who listened intently to them for a change. Of course, these self-introductions took up most of our first two-hour class, but the bonds we began to form, I hoped, were worth the investment. Towards the end of class, I distributed copies of the course syllabus, which included our course objectives, required readings, weekly class themes and assignments, class projects, evaluation criteria, and, my policy on absences and late arrivals. The syllabus was presented in a format that the students had never seen before. This was clearly a surprise for them, but my absence and lateness policies really grabbed their attention.

I stated that any more than two absences would lower the student's grade for the course and arriving more than thirty minutes late for any class would constitute an absence. These were standards Shelly and I had used effectively in other courses, to encourage active student participation and discourage slackers from remaining in our classes. What we hadn't bargained on were the deeply-held cultural assumptions we were contradicting in this code of conduct. By being so firm, we were marching against the tide of leniency that had been swamping public education in Bucharest.

The education sector in Romania was deeply affected by the major social changes that were then occurring. The 1990s constituted a cooling-off period for the entire country after years of rigid, tyrannical directives from Romanian central authorities during the long Communist era. The freedom unleashed by the 1989 revolution had caused educators to allow students autonomy, to become involved when it suited them and only to the extent they deemed necessary for their individual needs. In mainstream academic programs, students were attending classes as often as they wanted, or not at all, provided they managed to pass the final oral and written exams. This was how I remembered educational practices in France from my year at university there. We were requiring something completely different.

It was challenging to uphold these standards. We had to explicitly state and restate to our deans our firm belief that employing strict but fair rules would benefit our students in learning and developing

professional skills. We argued that they would end up more employ-
able among the multinational corporations and non-governmental
organizations that were then sprouting like wildflowers in Bucharest.
Indeed, many well-known organizations, such as Citibank, IBM, and
McDonald's, were just discovering the ripe new market that Romania
was offering them. After years of isolation, the country was working
hard to integrate its markets with those of its trading partners to the
West, rather than the East. Romania was also a substantial market for
outside investors. Its population of 19.2 million people was the second
largest population in Eastern Europe, after Poland[35]. In fact, the population was larger by a few million people when we were there than it
is now, due to substantial emigration by Romanians to other parts of
the European Union.

Our intent as visiting educators was to link our classrooms where
we served as cultural role models to the real world beyond them.
Whenever we could, we tried to share with our students our experiences
we'd acquired from living and working in the U.S. and other cultures,
so they could apply new ideas to their own lives. Our travel-deprived
students, locked until recently in a repressive society shut off from the
outside world, were a captive and interested audience, especially at the
onset, when our novelty value as Americans was still extremely high.

Both Shelly and I started pinpointing highly motivated students who
seemed to be drawn to us as their potential mentors. During our two
years in Bucharest, we recommended many of them for international
study programs, ranging from short courses at Central European
University in Budapest, which enjoyed the strong support of George
Soros, to longer graduate study programs in E.U. countries and the
United States.

One of these students sat near the front of my class. In classroom
discussions, Cosmina was quick to offer her opinions, which often di-

verged from the class consensus, but showed originality of thought. As she neared her graduation date, she shared with me her hopes of studying criminology at a graduate school in the United States. As I'd done for several other students, I sat with her and worked through her personal statement, which was required by most American graduate programs. She was not shy about self-promotion, which had at times led to her social ostracism among her peers. For me, though, it represented a new attitude that was taking hold among a small group of young people who seemed likely to lead the charge toward liberalization.

Romania's younger generation was grappling with the concept of self-promotion to further their professional lives. As a rule, our students were living with parents and older siblings for whom the State had dictated their lives; they had been expected to obey authority figures without questioning them. Family ties were strong; children weren't expected to challenge the decisions of their elders. Some were beginning to do so, and the stakes were high and stressful to those involved. In that period of serious reinvention for the country, forces were conspiring to upset many of the traditional beliefs and practices. Practically overnight, employment prospects turned dismal for middle-aged and older Romanians who had previously worked as civil servants and factory laborers. State-run operations were rapidly being shuttered and factory production was no longer competitive with production plants with higher technology in neighboring E.U. countries.

A widespread assumption among younger Romanians was that anyone over thirty-five had been hopelessly corrupted by the old regime and couldn't be re-educated for the new era of freewheeling capitalism. This prejudice was based on the way many private citizens served as informants of the *Securitate*, or Romanian secret police, during the earlier Communist era. At its height in the 1980s, the *Securitate* employed some 11,000 agents and had a half-million unpaid informants. Under Ceaușescu, it had been one of the most brutal secret police forces in the world, responsible for the arrests, torture, and deaths of thousands of people.[36]

In contrast to the bright prospects of hard-working young adults, the future for many pensioners in Bucharest was dark. Nobody wanted to remember the distressing old days of Communism when nearly everyone had to strike a deal with the devil just to survive the hardships. Many older people were constantly reminded of their previous misdeeds. Many from that generation were forced to give up their apartments and move in with their adult children, owing to their severe penury. Others moved back to their hometowns in the country, where they could at least grow their own food on small plots, as many had done during the long years of shortages. The most unfortunate of all were left to eke out an existence on scraps taken from city refuse bins and beg at frigid street corners or subway stations.

The path of opportunity for the younger generation would travel directly through the consumer goods and service sectors. These areas were fast developing, along with the promotion of public demand for previously unavailable consumer items. Other key aspects of the emerging, new economy included the possibility of disposable income, a desire for a new lifestyle, and perhaps most importantly, knowledge of the English language. Our students were eager to improve their already strong language skills. Compared to the educated young people we had met in Asia, those in Bucharest achieved a higher level of speaking proficiency in English and they simply needed to adapt their rather technical spoken vocabularies to more everyday situations.

Their English writing skills weren't as good. Our Romanian students were less knowledgeable of English grammar than our Asian students had been. The Romanians also lacked basic sentence organization and syntax. Improving their writing skills was a constant challenge for Shelly and me. We tried to promote fundamental writing skills, focusing on crafting a clear topic sentence, well organized main points with supporting evidence, and a well-stated conclusion.

———

Living conditions on the city streets of Bucharest varied dramatically from season to season. The cooler months could be especially gloomy.

In October, just two months after Shelly and I arrived in Romania, a heavy cloud cover descended upon the city, bringing with it falling temperatures and a thick gray haze. By late November, we were well established in our daily winter routine, putting on heavy navy-blue down jackets, stocking caps, knee-high boots, and gloves over the professorial suits we wore to work. For the next six months, we stoically endured the dispiriting lack of sunshine that frequently prevailed.

The sun finally returned in early April and transformed the city almost overnight from a drab winter-land to a glorious spring. Daily temperatures soared from around five degrees centigrade (upper thirty degrees F) to nearly twenty-five degrees centigrade (around eighty degrees F). The super-short spring was swiftly followed by summer. Boilers in buildings were ill equipped to adapt to such sudden change. They had been time-set to continue generating heat until at least mid-April, and it seemed they couldn't be recalibrated for an unknown reason. We sweltered for days, indoors and out.

This same thing occurred, but in reverse, during the transition from autumn to the bitter cold of the Romanian winter. The boilers in most buildings had been pre-set to start up around mid-November and not before, even though the deep chill had already set in by then. For a few weeks that first fall in Bucharest, my students and I were shivering during our classes. There were times when Shelly and I and our students carried blankets to class and wore gloves indoors to ward off the cold temperatures. Trying to stay focused on our lecture topics was doubly difficult when we were all freezing.

On the other hand, Romanian summers were wonderful, so glorious that it was hard to imagine the darker periods of winter during those blessedly happy months. The sunlight of summer days extended from early morning until well past ten o'clock at night for a few precious months. Windows were thrown open to invite the fresh air indoors, and flowers bloomed in multitudes. Large numbers of Bucharest residents spent long hours lounging in outdoor cafes and camping out in city parks and on the beach along the Black Sea Coast. Herastrau Park, especially, became a wonderland of happy families out for strolls, urban dwellers dipping their toes in the refreshing lake, and office workers playing hooky and napping on park benches. When nightfall arrived, a host of lakefront cafes and bars extended their warm welcomes to legions of late-night merry-makers amidst the cheery fairy lights that twinkled in the nearby trees. It seemed that Romania had a bi-polar climate that affected the very mood and rhythm of its cities. These moods varied dramatically according to the seasons.

The nineties were a time of upheaval for many Romanians, and of course the citizens of Bucharest felt this displacement dramatically. During November of our first year in Romania, Shelly and I volunteered to serve as elections monitors for the country's second round of general elections, during which the country made its first moves towards democracy in more than 800 years! Over the centuries, Romania had undergone many different identities under widely differing foreign rulers—whose one common point was their authoritarian nature, whether they were Turkish pashas, Austro-Hungarian emperors, or Soviet First Secretaries.

The Romanians had endured all manner of heavy-handed rule and had emerged bruised but unbroken. Finally, Romanian citizens would be choosing their own leader in their own democratic national elections. In that year, the two leading candidates were the former Communist Party Chief Ion Iliescu on the left, who was still a strong proponent of State control over most sectors of society, and University of Bucharest Professor Emil Constantinescu, who represented the right and the profound change desired by Westward-leaning Romanian youth.

OSI was in the thick of preparations to ensure that these elections would follow established international protocols for free and fair procedures. It was managing both the preparation of election-monitoring materials and the training for those who wanted to volunteer as international election observers. At our first training session, we were given a packet of materials printed in English; they appeared quite professional and easy to follow, to my untrained eye. Our group of CEP Fellows was actively involved in this project, which included several evening preparation meetings at OSI's headquarters in advance of the elections and then finally a long weekend spent in the Transylvania town of Cluj-Napoca (called simply *Cluj*), where we were assigned to visit and observe numerous nearby polling precincts.

Our election-monitoring trainer was a recent graduate of the Faculty of Political Science at the University of Bucharest. Mihai hailed from Cluj. He was highly motivated and very accessible and seemed to possess the spirit of altruism and optimism that prevailed at the time. He was also a very skilled communicator, which was not uncommon among Transylvania natives who were exposed in daily life to many languages besides Romanian, including Hungarian, German, French, and English. The quirks of history had brought many ethnicities to that region to settle, which lent it a cosmopolitan veneer, especially in the larger cities. Of course, once you drove out to the countryside where more traditional lifestyles prevailed, it wasn't that different from other rural parts of Romania. What linked nearly all Romanians at that time was their unfamiliarity with the idea of citizen participation in government. Guidance would come from a small cadre of urban elites and intellectuals in Bucharest.

This new elite was in close contact with their peers in other Eastern European countries, among them the Czech Republic, Hungary, and Poland. These countries had conducted mostly successful national elections and were farther down the road towards membership in the European Union than Romania was. Despite the national mood of historic change and openness, a tight-knit group in the capital city was directing the nation's evolutionary development.

—————

Our group of election monitors headed out by van from Bucharest to Cluj one Friday evening. The weather at first appeared threatening, but finally settled into a cloudy and cold holding pattern. We arrived near midnight at the local inn where we'd be staying. Cluj was noted for its civic pride, and during that weekend, it clearly showed. The carefully preserved historic areas were neatly swept and the brisk pace of life had an undeniably Germanic beat, even though many of German origin had abandoned their homes in Romania and moved back to their newly liberated hometowns in Eastern Germany after the fall of the Berlin Wall.

We got an early start the next morning, after a breakfast of strong coffee, rolls, and cheese. It was a brisk Saturday morning, and our task was to tour the election precincts we were slated to monitor the next day as the ballots were cast and tabulated. Romania, like many other countries, scheduled its elections for a Sunday, to ensure a good turnout. Our assigned precincts were evenly divided between urban and rural locations.

In the city of Cluj, municipal government offices and public elementary and secondary schools had been designated as polling places for citizens living nearby. For the most part, the election booths in these locations had already been constructed, and they generally numbered between fifteen and twenty. The large official ballot boxes had been delivered to these urban locations. These boxes would hold all the cast ballots and at the end of Election Day would be carefully sealed and delivered to the regional precinct headquarters.

In the rural precincts in Transylvania, the situation was markedly different. While the types of polling places were like those in the cities, we discovered that the pace of preparation was slower in the countryside. When we visited the polling places, workers were still hammering away, building the booths. Mihai and several of the OSI representatives had to urge them to work faster, emphasizing that the people's voices needed to be heard and that international observers (meaning us) were watching.

The official ballot boxes hadn't yet arrived at several sites that Saturday afternoon, which was a serious concern for Mihai and his colleagues. They had to make several calls on their large, unwieldy mobile phones to confirm the time when the boxes might arrive. We understood the vastness and the relative isolation of the Romanian countryside during our tour. We later learned that the final election preparations ended up taking until late that Saturday night, just hours before the polling places were scheduled to open Sunday morning.

Mihai invited everyone in our monitoring group to a special home-cooked meal at his grandparents' estate in Cluj that Saturday evening. It was a very real treat after the cold, rigorous day of polling inspections. Stepping into the large, candlelit dining room felt like we were traveling back in time to the early 20ᵗʰ-century days of independence and national pride for these fiercely independent Transylvanians. Besides our group of eight observers, the dinner party included Mihai's brother and sister, his parents, and his paternal grandparents.

The long hardwood dining table easily accommodated us all. It was lavishly set and festooned with an autumnal centerpiece placed atop a hand-knitted black and red tablecloth in the finest Romanian tradition. Foods were delivered in white porcelain filigreed serving dishes or on long silver platters. The dinner courses started coming as soon as we all took a seat and they didn't stop coming for several hours.

The selections seemed to evolve organically from marinated mushrooms and pickles at the start to heavier fare, such as roast beef and chicken and oven-roasted potatoes, followed by stuffed bell peppers and hot baked bread, accompanied by *vinete*, a savory and spicy Romanian winter spread. Tasty Transylvanian white wines were flowing generously throughout our meal. The final course was a large baked wild berry pastry, topped with real cream and served with a local brandy. It was as hearty as it sounds and warmed us all considerably on that wintry evening. We finally bade our farewells late that evening after many boisterous toasts and found our way back to our inn and a deep slumber.

Sunday morning, we again headed out early, into an even colder, drizzlier day, visiting the very same polling stations we had on Saturday. This time, though, we wore our International Election Monitor badges around our necks and we walked with a seriousness of purpose. From the earliest polls we visited at eight o'clock that morning until the final polling centers where we lingered until around seven o'clock, we were on the alert for any polling irregularities. At first, these were few and far between, especially in downtown Cluj locations. Some polls were late to open, with long queues stretching out the door and down the block when we arrived. However, once all polling officials had arrived and took their position at their posts, the voting process began in earnest and continued steadily throughout the morning in the city.

We headed to the rural polling centers after lunch. Once again, it seemed the farther afield we traveled from our urban base, the more unusual the events we witnessed. Romanians are by nature sociable people, and this was especially evident at the rural locations. At one center, for example, large groups of Romanian men were standing near the entrance, talking animatedly as we approached them. One offered each of us shots of what looked like moonshine. It was apparent that he and a few others were already giddy and inebriated, and they were expecting even more merriment from this special event. We had to politely decline, considering the serious nature of our visit. We headed on towards the center, where voting appeared to be in full swing. Unfortunately, we soon clearly sensed that many voters were making their decisions with less-than-clear minds.

Near the main entrance of the polling place, we spotted several signs for different political parties and candidates, a clear violation of voting rules that mandated a distance of at least one hundred meters for any campaign-related materials. Before we could mention this to the officials in charge, we saw entire Romanian families entering voting booths together to cast multiple ballots. The heads of these families were deciding for the other individuals in their clans eligible to vote.

This behavior sent a clear signal that the Romanian patriarchic traditions were deeply ingrained in the voters' minds and were affecting their voting attitudes and behaviors. This contradicted the rules for free and fair voting procedures, but one election was not likely to change such long—established cultural norms overnight. At this poll, we witnessed clear violations of the one person, one vote rule that was a pre-requisite for open and democratic elections.

As we tried to explain our numerous concerns to the precinct staff, we noticed that certain candidate names had been carved into the wooden beams that constituted the frames for the voting booths, another violation of established procedures that prohibited favoritism towards any individual candidate at the actual voting centers. Without even looking for violations, in just a few short minutes, we'd identified four major missteps from standard operating procedures for truly democratic elections. Not surprisingly, the next day we learned that some of the actual voting boxes from the rural polling stations never arrived at the regional polling centers for tabulation after the polls closed. They had simply vanished, never to be found.

A key lesson we all learned was that an entire country couldn't be expected to adapt to externally imposed values and codes of conduct in the short run, no matter how passionately the proponents of change wished for it. Democratic change might be implemented eventually in Romania, but the people fastest to accept and adhere to these changes would be the educated urban classes, while people in rural towns would follow slowly. In the end, the forces of change represented by candidate Constantinescu prevailed. Whether the numerous irregularities in many rural voting locations affected the outcome is difficult to say, but it seems unlikely, since the professor's win was by a large margin and provoked a massive celebration in the country's large cities. This represented the first truly peaceful transfer of power in the country since the violent overthrow of the dictator several years earlier.

———•———

After the election, Shelly and I settled into our teaching routines in earnest and before long, the winter holidays were upon us. As in many European countries, the universities in Romania provided faculty, students, and most staff members a lengthy break over the Christmas holidays. We took advantage of that and made an extended trip to Cyprus. The island is strategically important in the Eastern Mediterranean. Its Greek, Roman, and medieval ruins attest to the fact that the island has been a crossroads for many civilizations over the centuries. Even more importantly for us, after enduring so much darkness and damp, bitter cold, the southerly location provided a wonderful reprieve. It was still a little chilly there, but the climate in Cyprus stayed sunny for nearly our entire two-week stay. When it was time to return to Bucharest, we were both feeling refreshed and raring to go again.

Our positive energy came in handy, since final exams were scheduled for the end of January. Shelly and I had wisely assigned team-based, case study projects to our students as their final projects. We were about the only faculty members among hundreds at ASE who had bucked the trend of planning essay examinations covering the required course readings, as prescribed by the school administration.

These final projects were intended to be practical and relevant to our students' lives. We recommended that they conduct in-depth research of either a multinational corporation or international non-governmental organization with offices in Bucharest. Since I had sixty students and Shelly had about one hundred in our respective International Management classes, divvying up our students into project teams was an attempt to save ourselves from an avalanche of final paperwork during the grading period. We'd managed to reduce the total number of final papers we needed to grade to fifteen for me and twenty-five for her. The projects required oral presentations by each student team, so we had to coach all of them on how to organize their presentations, how to share work tasks fairly, how to construct a Power Point (a fairly new technology then) presentation, and how to engage their audience, all important communication skills and completely new to nearly all of them.

This method of student evaluation proved to be very popular among our students. Several teams in both our classes focused on the mission, structure, and operations of either the European Union (EU) or the North Atlantic Treaty Organization (NATO). Young people in Bucharest were strongly in favor of joining both groups at the earliest possible opportunity, but few could say precisely why or how their country might benefit from belonging. Our students had a general sense that membership in these organizations might come soon, and they were very eager to have their country more integrated with their E.U.-member neighbors. In fact, Romania didn't join NATO until 2004, and the European Union until 2007, owing to the usual bureaucratic delays that occur within international organizations.[37] No doubt, these must have disappointed them immensely.

Some of the earliest multinational corporate investors in Romania during the transition period from Communism to capitalism were from the so-called sin sector. Cigarette companies such as Philip Morris and R.J. Reynolds were big employers of hard-working young Romanian employees. The same was true for beer manufacturers, such as Tuborg and Heineken, which had large plants employing many Romanian factory workers. Many of our students felt very fortunate to acquire internships and, eventually, professional positions with these companies. All these firms, as well as giant consumer brands companies such as Proctor and Gamble, Colgate Palmolive, and Coca Cola, were popular organizations to study for our students' final projects. Both Shelly and I became experts on these organizations, several of which would become our corporate clients during our second year in Romania.

For the students in my smaller Economic Case Studies class, the focus of our final projects was a different one. Considering how isolated Romania had been from the global marketplace for decades, I assigned the project teams in that class to do country profiles for potential investors. I tried to suggest medium-sized countries, to enhance the probability that any lessons learned might also apply to the economic and social challenges facing Romania.

Our teams ended up presenting and writing about Malaysia, Ivory Coast, Venezuela, Bulgaria, and South Korea, all of which had experienced growing pains of their own in the 1980s or early 1990s. Students discussed and learned about critical economic issues related to these countries, including their high rates of unemployment, limited natural resources, and undereducated workforces. It became clear to them that Romania was in no way unique in terms of its slow pace towards national development.

The spring term seemed to include so many outreach events that I can hardly remember the physical act of teaching my regular classes. Among the many gripping extracurricular events that took place in just four short months was a Balkan Student Debate involving students from six Central and Eastern European nations, including the host country of Romania. Shelly and I served as coaches of the four participating Romanian collegiate teams in the run-up to the event and then as judges at the one-day event held at ASE. The debate theme focused on the pros and cons of E.U. membership. The event was hugely popular and attracted considerable media attention. We were interviewed by, and quoted in, several daily Bucharest newspapers.

Another important event that semester was a collaborative teaching strategies conference that included all CEP lecturers from Eastern Europe as presenters. Our group traveled together by train to Hungary for this. We had opportunities to speak with our peers about how we were applying active learning in our classrooms. This was a first-of-its kind professional development event for the region, as teaching methods that weren't teacher-centered were still unknown in Central and Eastern Europe. Not to overstate it, but we were acting as *de facto* educational revolutionaries, bringing radical new approaches to our local colleagues and students. As with any revolution, there were strong sentiments against our methods among the proponents of the *status quo*, and we attempted to ride out the storm as best we could.

Shelly and I presented together on our methods for student debates in our management classes and how they could be adapted for use in any undergraduate social science class in Eastern Europe. The conference proceedings were published in a special journal that was widely read among development organizations and future-oriented educators in the region.

Around this time, I began conducting training workshops at the Center for Independent Journalism, a non-profit organization committed to "promoting free and independent media in Eastern and Central Europe."[38] This was very rewarding. I could draw upon the skills I had acquired and used in my days as a reporter and editor for *The Economist* in New York and Tokyo. Like many Western-trained journalists of that era, I had often taken the existence of a free and independent press for granted in my years of reporting. I had to adjust these assumptions to the hard reality of the media in Bucharest in the 1990s, much of which was still State-controlled or influenced.

Prior to 1990, most working journalists had been co-opted by the Romanian State. All messages emanating from the print and broadcast media had been vetted by State authorities. In the media, as in other sectors, those affiliated with the old regime were considered tainted in the new era. The journalists who followed were all raw recruits, with very little Western training or ideas. Initially, they showed no evidence of knowing how to conduct an interview that considered different sides of an issue. They also needed basic training on the nuts and bolts of objective reporting.

There were also the nagging rules of professional writing that most of these aspiring journalists seemed unaware of, including how to write a short but poignant news headline, how to preview or foreshadow important points, how to cite sources appropriately, and how to provide research data or statistics to validate or enhance key story ideas and arguments. We plowed ahead as best we could in sessions that were invariably too short for them to take in and apply, especially with so many new concepts and working tools. A few of them caught on quickly and for the others I could only hope they would receive additional training.

I applied some of my own skills at a newly launched English language magazine about Romania entitled *In Review Romania*. I was named associate editor, and my primary duty was to track the week's most important news stories and summarize them for distribution via the Internet. This provided access to Romania-related information to international subscribers who had previously lacked it. We received email queries from Europe, the United States, and even Asia. This was also my first experience in reporting and communicating on news events via the Internet, which was still in its earliest stages, but poised to grow exponentially.

At the end of our first academic year as CEP Fellows, Shelly and I had time over the summer to try our hand at consulting for the growing list of American-owned and other multinational enterprises in Bucharest. Both of us had made contacts with several of these organizations while looking for internships for our best undergraduate students. We had taught and trained our designated interns, providing them with important skills valued by Western organizations, among them improved business English for work situations, problem-solving abilities, public speaking skills, and clear business writing.

Corporate managers started contacting us directly, wanting us to train their employees as we had been doing in our ASE classes. Through a variety of appointments that evolved into a sort of needs assessment of the international business sector in Bucharest, we were able to identify certain critical needs for Western businesses *vis-à-vis* their local employees. We then set to work constructing a product line of professional training materials and services. By our second autumn in the country, we began conducting specialized workshops for Romanian employees of foreign enterprises.

During our second year at ASE, we were fully engaged in our university lives and in our parallel world as international business consultants. Our first and consistently most popular training workshop for new corporate clients focused on fostering improved communication and teambuilding skills among their junior and mid-level employees. We also did workshops on themes such as marketing to clients, conflict resolution, and negotiating for success. Overall, however, the teambuilding training was how we made our mark and, for a time, earned a minor degree of fame in Bucharest.

Our two-day workshops, normally conducted on a Friday and

Saturday, achieved best results when performed at a client's off-site training or retreat center. The ten to fifteen managers selected to participate were from the sales and marketing staffs, since most foreign products at the time in Romania were consumer-oriented and linked to brand image and direct appeals to potential buyers. Our clients were hoping to construct a new consumer mindset within a Romanian public that had for generations lived in a marketplace of scarcity. This required staff members who were good, confident communicators, as well as highly motivated and energetic, since they worked long hours. The public had to be told precisely why new consumer products were good for them and capable of enhancing their quality of life. These corporate employees needed to discover ways to go the extra mile each working day, since the competition for a foothold in the newly emerging market was fierce.

The expectation that these young employees at Western enterprises should be internally driven was completely alien to the norms of Romanian culture. It had been imported from the West, where individualistic attitudes were more prevalent. We were the facilitators of this transformation among our workshop participants. The huge challenge we faced was that Romanian culture hadn't previously valued individuals who were willing to speak up and make their plans known. Practically overnight, multinational employers were expecting to assess and compensate this new breed of individual according to their levels of success or failure in meeting performance benchmarks.

Our workshops focused heavily on cross-cultural management themes. At the time, we felt that certain models were especially useful for an international workplace culture undergoing profound transformation. These themes, explained via popular Western management theories, were our focus on day one of our workshops. Three models, especially, seemed to capture everyone's attention again and again.

The first, Maslow's hierarchy of human needs,[39] explained how an individual's basic physical needs for survival evolved into higher-order social and self-development needs once they were satisfied. Romanian employees, unlike their parents, were moving beyond basic survival goals and towards more sophisticated life plans. The second, Hofstede's management dimensions of culture[40], including the key categories of power distance and uncertainty avoidance, demonstrated how different employee perceptions could be found within the same multinational enterprises. The third, the Johari Window model of management self-perceptions versus perceptions by others,[41] emphasized the importance of active listening and asking for feedback from peers, superiors, and subordinates.

These fundamental theories of corporate culture and effective communication at the workplace provided us the opportunity to establish our credibility with our trainees early on, which then allowed us to pursue higher-risk activities later. On day two, we moved on to more participatory activities, such as simulations of business meetings and negotiations with clients. We role-played workplace incidents that caused friction between management and workers, often called critical incidents. We also taught methods of giving and receiving performance evaluations in the context of a manager-employee interview.

All these active learning tasks were eye-openers for our Romanian participants, requiring them to use English in ways they may never have used previously. They also had to behave in front of their peers with a willingness to make mistakes and learn from them. Considering they'd chosen to work for Western employers and wanted to get ahead in their jobs, the overwhelming majority was willing to do their best and benefited accordingly.

After two years in Romania, Shelly and I realized that we were developing into first-class educators and corporate trainers. We'd faced and met many tough challenges in the classroom and the private sector in Bucharest. We were also building a viable consulting business in an intriguing, newly emerging developing country. At the end of the day, though, we both knew that our courses and training workshops involved a lot of trial and error that could be avoided through further education and training. Moreover, although we were impressed by the efforts being made by a new generation of Romanian nation-builders, we knew the payoff would be many years in the making. We weren't willing or able to wait that long.

Our time in Asia had lit a spark that we knew we had to keep burning as we looked to the future. Even then, many were speaking of the coming 21st century as an era of Asian ascendancy. To enhance our chances of being a part of this dynamic new period in Asia, we began researching U.S. graduate programs based in California that might provide us with opportunities for Asia-based research, as well as substantive adult teaching and learning methods that would fortify us as cross-cultural educators.

Our choice for re-entering the academic world after more than a decade away was the University of Southern California (USC) in Los Angeles. After reviewing the catalogues of many graduate schools at the Fulbright Foundation in Bucharest, taking the requisite Graduate Record Examination (GRE) there—which wasn't easy after years of real-world experience—and completing the other required application materials, we sent off our applications by registered mail, sat back, and waited. Within a month, we learned that USC had accepted us.

We were thrilled by the idea of returning to school in mid-career. From what we'd already learned, we were convinced that USC could meet our needs with its graduate program in international education. It would educate us about the most pressing educational issues in the developing world. It also seemed possible that we could both gain teaching assistantships at the school, which would upgrade our English-language teaching abilities while enhancing the language proficiency and study skills of foreign students coming to USC. This graduate program seemed to offer a perfect match for our professional needs while offering us the chance to dedicate ourselves in a way that would lessen the shock of returning to live in the U.S. full-time. In that regard, we weren't disappointed. The coming years turned out to be a period of renewed energy and nearly unlimited curiosity.

4: Los Angeles, CA

He who would have the fruit must climb the tree. – An American Proverb

We moved to Los Angeles from Bucharest in the late 1990s with a mixture of excitement, relief, and trepidation. While greatly looking forward to our return to academic life and a warmer climate, we weren't sure what life would be like for two mid-life students in the classroom. These worries turned out to be unfounded. Our transition went far better than expected.

As we deplaned at Los Angeles International Airport (LAX) after a marathon overnight flight from Bucharest via Paris once again, our conception of the L.A. awaiting us was still a simplified one. We hadn't spent much time there previously, so we discovered a culture new to us. Downtown Los Angeles, where USC's historic campus is located, was virtually unknown to us. The little we'd seen of L.A.'s urban core had involved driving through it on the way to other places. From what we'd read about downtown in the *Los Angeles Times* and had seen on Southern California television news, the area appeared to be an overflowing pot of ethnic groups, causing unmanageable urban tensions. In fact, at this time, downtown L.A. was still attempting to overcome all the notoriety it had earned from the riots of 1992 that shocked the world.

Ready or not, we were about to become California residents. We expected our graduate program of study to last, at most, three or four years. It ended up taking us six to complete all the required coursework and research, which we didn't mind, as we were constantly marveling at all the city had to offer. Much of our previous adult lives in the United States had occurred on the East Coast, whose residents tended to cast a wary eye towards the unorthodox lifestyles and left-leaning politics of the "Left Coast."[42] We saw California in much that way, at least when we first arrived.

It was odd once again to have the vantage point of university students after so many years spent in the real world. Shelly and I were entering USC as doctoral students with well-developed plans of what we hoped to achieve. These converged in our desire to better understand educational theories and methods suited to diverse student populations. We felt this could be at least partially accomplished by pursuing teaching assistantships at the American Language Institute (ALI), where many foreign students were required to enroll prior to joining their full-time academic degree programs. Many of our peers in our graduate program at the School of Education were already working there, which provided them with full tuition scholarships and a reasonable monthly paycheck.

A major fly in the ointment, though, was the fact that we'd arrived at campus too late to be considered for ALI teaching positions that first year on campus. Course enrollments and teaching assignments had been finalized before we'd departed Bucharest. It looked as though we'd have to scramble to find some sort of gainful employment to pay for our graduate studies.

We explained all this to our faculty advisor, Dr. William Rideout, at our first meeting in his office on campus at Waite Philips Hall. He listened carefully, smiled sympathetically, and told us not to worry. He had, no doubt, counseled many other graduate students in this type of situation. He invited us on an informal walking tour of our new base of operations in Waite Philips. We visited the various departments in the School of Education that stretched over several floors. As we were nearing the end of our tour, we paused next to a large picture window on the building's top floor. While admiring the panoramic views of campus and downtown L.A., Dr. Rideout casually mentioned that he knew of a graduate assistantship that had recently become vacant in the Center of Higher Education Research just a few floors below. He felt I might be the right candidate and offered to put in a good word with the professor in charge of the center. As for Shelly, he said he knew several USC alumni working at nearby universities, and he would check with them about available positions for her.

Within two weeks of that meeting, I'd begun working at the center and Shelly had been hired to work in a women's leadership office at a college near USC. We had just learned an important lesson about academic culture. When one opportunity dried up, another would present itself if you had the right personal connections. This resonated with what we'd learned earlier about surviving in Tokyo. Ironically, our good friend Dr. Bill Gay, whom we'd met in Tokyo, had taught at USC for many years and had recommended us to this very program. Bill would play an important role later in encouraging his own protégée, Dr. David Eskey, the Director of ALI, to hire us.

Shelly and I quickly realized that our personal allies would provide us with access to rewarding work. Later, they would be consequential in supporting our efforts to gain critical faculty support and research grants for our field research projects abroad. Without them, we never would have experienced the amazing period of professional development that we enjoyed in L.A. The university, like us, was undergoing an important period of transition at the time. It was moving away from its traditional identity as a commuter school catering to a student body hailing mostly from Southern California. Its new identity would be that of a global research university comprised of the highest percentage of international students at any major American university. USC would hold that impressive distinction for thirteen years running.[43]

USC was especially effective in recruiting students from East Asia and South Asia because it had established branch offices in several important Asian capitals, among them Seoul, Tokyo, and Taipei. USC eventually established other Asian recruiting offices in Shanghai and Beijing, as well as in Southeast Asia. As for Shelly and me, we were trying to jump-start our U.S.-based careers and lifestyles after ten years living abroad in Asia and Eastern Europe. Fortunately for us, our new graduate school program, professors, and colleagues seemed to appreciate and value our overseas experiences, to which we referred again and again during in-class discussions and project assignments. We were grateful to have such a deep pool to draw from.

————•————

From the start, we mingled with individuals interested in international affairs. We discussed key global educational and development issues that demanded critical thought. One of our early courses in the program was Foundations of International Education. It illuminated the stark educational disparities that existed between developed and developing countries, in terms of student outcomes and dropout rates. We learned that while a large majority of students in wealthy countries finished high school and went on to college, this was not the case in most poor countries, where a lot of young people didn't even make the jump from elementary to junior high school. Having experienced the optimism of Peace Corps volunteers in Thailand, our new knowledge seemed to be throwing cold water on development program efforts to reduce social and economic inequalities around the world.

There was a similarly discouraging gap in educational achievements for male versus female students at all levels. In virtually every region of the world, male students outperformed females in terms of their level of educational attainment. That has changed somewhat in the ensuing years, but back then low-income girls were more likely than boys to drop out of school to care for younger siblings or to generate supplemental income for their struggling families. These gender differences were also linked to literacy rates. Women were consistently more likely to be illiterate than men in the developing world.

This sobering picture galvanized us to focus on the serious educational inequalities that existed everywhere, even in the United States. We compared the performance of U.S. students by racial category, in terms of scores achieved by high school students on standardized tests such as the Scholastic Aptitude Test (SAT) and the American College Testing (ACT) in Math, Reading and Science. Test results showed that Asian and white students consistently scored the highest, and at nearly equivalent levels, followed by Hispanic students and then African-American students.[44]

Lively debates broke out during class, with our professor Dr. Nelly Stromquist and the rest of us offering a variety of plausible explanations for such racial gaps. We agreed that lower incomes negatively affected student test performance. Some classmates suggested that U.S. social inequalities dated to the era of slavery and were a direct result of that history. Others felt that attitudes towards formal academic study varied among different U.S. sub-cultures and depended on the perceived value of such study. Related to this, another negative factor was the crowded and noisy living conditions experienced by young students living in inner city housing. Difficult home situations led to distracted or disappointed students.

We all benefited from the diverse enrollment in our graduate class, which helped us develop a keener understanding of the real-life realities of varying ethnic groups. It was also beneficial in studying the influence that gender had on individual perceptions of the importance and utility of formal schooling. In the U.S., male students are increasingly turning away from higher education, while female enrollments continue to rise. Young adult males are increasingly feeling a sense of alienation from America's higher education—and the ramifications for American society are now being felt.

Our circle of close friends represented diverse national and ethnic backgrounds. It included a Taiwanese couple, several Hispanic women, a few white Americans who like us had lived abroad, a pair of Turkish exchange students, a Moroccan man, and a Native American man. Inevitably, in our conversations, we had dramatically differing perspectives about educational priorities and the best policies to pursue them and encourage better academic achievement for students of all ethnic backgrounds.

These discussions of U.S. student performance among low-income minority students became closely linked to the real world when Shelly and I volunteered as after-school instructors for USC's Neighborhood Academic Initiative (NAI). NAI had been striving to build bridges between the university and neighboring public schools in the University Park section of Los Angeles. This area was largely low income and Hispanic or African-American. Earlier, the university had received strong criticism for being a white enclave in what was essentially a very diverse inner city.

The program aimed to improve the academic skills of neighborhood public school students, especially in reading, writing, and math. Groups of junior high school students were matched with older tutors and academic mentors drawn from the USC student population. Another special focus was to encourage the young participants to become familiar with the academic context of learning that prevails at universities. NAI program activities took place on campus, in the mornings before school and immediately after school. In this way, the participants grew comfortable interacting with adults and their peers in a structured learning environment.

The organization's official mission was to serve as a rigorous, seven-year pre-college enrichment program designed to prepare low-income neighborhood students for admission to a college or university.[45] Probably the most impressive aspect was the promise that the students who stayed with the program for the long run, through junior and senior high school, would receive full scholarships to USC. This was no small matter, considering USC's sky-high tuition and fast-rising academic reputation.

To bolster the chances that NAI students would stick with the program for the duration, an agreement was signed between NAI organizers and the participants' parents and other key family members. This agreement stated that the family would participate regularly in Family

Development Institute meetings on Saturday mornings. Inner-city kids needed the strong support of their families to get ahead. Their families, in turn, needed assistance in better understanding how to foster a positive learning environment at home, how to solve conflicts, and how to communicate more proactively.

Shelly and I both enjoyed being volunteer mentors that first semester. We worked with a small group of six to eight junior high students who were almost evenly divided between Hispanics and African Americans. We assisted them with their English reading, writing, and oral presentation skills. NAI focused on recruiting students who were not already at the top of their classes, based on the assumption that the highest performing students would find a way to go on to college anyway.

NAI selected its junior high participants because they were mid-level performers, not the academic stars, in their classrooms. Most were earning B or C grades in school, but according to their teachers, they showed the potential to improve if provided with additional guidance and encouragement. In academic terms, this personalized support is called scaffolding, a term that invokes the image of a building structure that can survive and eventually thrive if provided with tangible external supports that can one day be removed. The same concept could be applied to these vulnerable youngsters.

We reviewed our students' textbooks for their English, Social Studies, and History classes. We urged them to think more deeply about the key themes, while also trying to relate school subjects to their own experiences. This was very similarly to what we'd recently been doing with our university students in Bucharest. Of course, our older Romanian students had possessed greater self-confidence than these youngsters. In Los Angeles, as we had earlier in Bucharest, we were discovering that by urging our students to speak as much as possible, both with each other and with us, they were slowly finding their inner voices. They became willing to express their opinions in public. This important skill might otherwise have remained dormant in them, considering the context of their everyday lives—their large class sizes at school, for example, and the heavy administrative workloads their teachers faced.

Our students' progress made it possible for them, even at the ages of twelve or thirteen, to make structured oral presentations to an audience. It was important for us to model key components of an effective speech, as we'd done in Bucharest. That starts with the choice of an interesting topic to talk about, the need to tell your audience what you'd be speaking about and why, and the positive impact on listeners that compelling examples could have. When they were ready, we worked together to draft simple PowerPoint slides that our mentees could use as visual aids during their presentations. Before our very eyes, the youngsters were acquiring useful skills that would serve as scaffolds for their academic progress in the years ahead, in high school and beyond.

———————

With all the excitement of a new academic life, it was hard to find the time needed to search for suitable lodgings. What we really wanted was, first and foremost, a convenient commute to USC, followed by a basic level of creature comfort and a decent security situation in our new neighborhood. What we ended up settling for in our first month in L.A. only met the first of these three criteria. The place wasn't a bad commute to USC. Basically, it was a fully furnished, one-bedroom apartment with an anonymous feel to it. Perfect for a stranger in a strange land, but not right for a couple settling back into our homeland.

We selected our initial housing complex from one of the free housing booklets we could find in the newspaper racks of Ralph's or Vons supermarkets. If we could have, we would have returned earlier to L.A. and compared different neighborhoods before choosing our housing more systematically. Unfortunately, our hectic final months in Bucharest had prevented us from doing that. We ended up deciding on a place to live based solely on cost, which is never an ideal situation. The required security deposit for our new unit was one month's rent, and the rent itself didn't exceed what our graduate student budget could support. The location, unfamiliar to us at the time we'd signed our rental agreement, was an area called the Westlake district on the Western edge of downtown L.A. We learned to describe it to friends as Silverlake-adjacent, which, we hoped, made them think of us living in a trendy urban retreat.

Dr. Rideout had suggested we should consider Silverlake to live in. He lived there in a beautiful California bungalow-style home located in the hills above the reservoir. We would have dearly loved to be neighbors, if only we could have swung it. Unfortunately, we had reverted to a miserly graduate student budget, at least until the dust settled. We couldn't consider buying a place of our own until we'd gotten firmly established in L.A.

That first apartment lacked personality, which was a real negative in terms of lifting our spirits after a long week of work combined with a huge amount of evening homework. We knew we needed to find something better. We would, as soon as we had the time and energy. One of the uncontrollable side effects of traveling as much as we did was that our furniture and other household items were scattered across two rental storage units and in family members' homes. It would take at least a month to consolidate it all in one place. Until then, we needed a furnished place to live in. We tried to convince ourselves that our new place was something special, considering it had a small plunge pool in the courtyard, a sun deck right next to it, and a few coin-operated washers and dryers down the sunny breezeway from our unit. These few amenities, in fact, looked pretty good to us after our gloom-infested Bucharest apartment, to which we'd never quite warmed up.

Even with the positive attitudes we strove to maintain towards our new L.A. digs, it was impossible to overlook the obvious security risks looming just outside our front door, which was in a rough-and-tumble neighborhood featuring pawnshops, liquor stores, Popeye's, and a 7-Eleven. The downtown L.A. of those days was still an urban frontier, with little hint yet of the renovated, hip, and more cleaned-up place that now attracts renowned artists and millionaires. It was marginalized and seedy, at least our corner of it was, with frequent shouting matches by the next-door neighbors and blaring alarms outside our bedroom window. These noises often interrupted normal daytime conversations and woke us in the wee hours.

Before long, we were counting the days until the end of our first and only month in Westlake. We vowed to relocate just as fast as we possibly could, gather all our things together, and move the little we had with us. We needed to find a nicer neighborhood where we could safely take walks to reduce the stresses of graduate school and have a restful place to chill out at the end of each day. Our new friends and colleagues advised us to look farther west for what we desired. It was in that direction that the best selection of available housing would await us. Northward would have taken us to Hollywood, which was quite a bit farther away from USC than where we presently lived. Southward offered even higher-density housing than what already seemed dangerous to us. Eastward rose the mammoth, high-rise buildings of downtown L.A. that were mostly commercial towers in that era.

We set out on a serious house hunt one Saturday morning in late September. We'd acquired a pre-owned minivan and were raring to go, with the intention of signing a lease that would begin the first day of October. After a few minutes' drive, we arrived on the outskirts of a huge section of mid-town Los Angeles that is better known as Koreatown. It extended north to south from Beverly Boulevard to Pico Boulevard and east to west from Hoover Avenue to Western Avenue. It has expanded even further in all directions since then. We noticed that most of the store signs quickly changed from English and Spanish in Westlake to English and Korean or just Korean as we crossed into Koreatown.

In certain parts of K-Town, as it is known locally, there were some very nice historic buildings and townhouses. Considering that this section of town provided great access along the 10 Freeway, Wilshire Boulevard, and Vermont Avenue to USC, downtown, and the booming West Side of L.A., we expected to find a great selection of potential rentals there. We were wrong. We could find very few signs announcing apartments to rent, perhaps because we didn't read Korean. We approached several buildings that looked promising and pressed the button for the rental office. To our dismay, we encountered several non-English speaking building managers or rental agents who simply waved us off with a gruff, "No!" or the Korean version of it, not even allowing us to ask questions about rental units or fill out a rental application.

This behavior unmistakably signaled a type of insular attitude towards outsiders, even in the heart of a cosmopolitan city like Los Angeles. Based on our prior travels and sensitivity to vocal intonations and body language, it was clear that at least some Korean residents wanted nothing to do with outsiders, even white academics. This wasn't a good sign, considering the race riots of only a few years earlier that involved Korean business owners and African-American customers. They had alarmed and alienated huge numbers of Angelinos. If Korean landlords were treating us so rudely, we wondered just how badly they were treating people of darker skin. I'm not sure even as I write much later, if this bunker mentality in K-Town has evolved into more tolerant attitudes towards outsiders or not. Our experience was distinctly negative, for two travel-tested, Asia-loving house hunters.

We drove further westward along Third Street, until we'd reached a very nice little neighborhood called Larchmont. This area was built around a two-block-long shopping strip with several nice restaurants, a drug store, bookshop, deli, and a few specialized boutiques. What seemed particularly attractive to us were the well-maintained single-family homes on either end of the strip. Their lawns were brilliant green and manicured, and their mid-century exteriors were attractive. This community in the Hancock Park section of Los Angeles had been a preferred location for many film industry moguls and stars in an earlier epoch, and it still exuded prosperity and a hint of glamor. It had been nicely cared for, as evidenced by the many mature trees in top condition and the paved sidewalks that offered a very pleasant stroll to residents and visitors alike. We were eager to live there in Larchmont and drove around inspecting it from every possible angle.

We stopped for lunch at Le Petit Greek, a popular restaurant located in the center of the activity. Shelly, having grown up in Greece, was partial to spinach pies, Greek salad, and strong Greek coffee. She was easily sold on Larchmont. Alas, housing costs were sky high, considering the prime location. Upon completing our meal, we reluctantly pushed on farther westward. By this time, we were feeling the enervating effects of a bountiful Greek meal. We started to steel ourselves mentally for additional days of house hunting that appeared inevitable. The afternoon was winding down as we drove on, still within the tree-lined neighborhoods of Hancock Park. Crossing over Highland Avenue, we noticed a few low-rise apartment buildings that appeared promising to two wandering scholars in need of a special haven. We were glad to see that dwellings in this area were ensconced in the shade of many sycamore trees that lined the residential streets. We noticed the well-tended lawns we craved in front of the buildings, with not even one abandoned shopping cart or discarded whiskey bottle in sight.

While slowing to admire the neighborhood, we spotted a sign above the entrance of one of the smaller historic buildings advertising a one-bedroom apartment for rent. This was it, or at least we sincerely hoped so! We quickly parked in front and confidently headed to the entrance, once again using our practiced cold-calling skills on the rental manager. Fortunately, the young lady whose job it was to take applications and manage the property was home when we rang the bell. She came to the front gate, introduced herself as Sophia, and led us across the brick-lined inner courtyard that formed the bottom level of the building structure.

This two-story building was exposed to the elements, not only in the main courtyard, but also at the entrances of the twenty apartments within the complex. The building's cornerstone near the entrance said that it dated to 1924. This made us reflect on the many aspiring actors and other glamor seekers of the silent film era who must have lived in this dwelling. Sophia told us right away that she was a recent film school graduate and an aspiring director. She later used her unit and the building exterior as props in a short film she co-wrote and directed. She smiled while taking our completed applications and informed us she'd be interviewing potential tenants the following morning at ten o'clock.

She wondered if we could come back and audition, or rather meet, with her. Without hesitation, we both replied in the affirmative and headed home with at least a glimmer of hope.

The following day, we returned a few minutes early for our appointment. As we entered the building, we noticed there were already nine or ten applicants lined up outside Sophia's apartment. Most were single and looked to be aspiring, film-industry types. Shelly and I stood out among them as bookish sorts. We reminded ourselves that we had an important point in our favor. We both had full-time jobs at well-known local colleges. We were confident this would convince Sophia of our likelihood to pay the rent punctually each month, compared to the others. Eavesdropping as we all took turns meeting with her, we could hear our competitors describing their latest film project or script ideas, none of which seemed to offer solid employment prospects beyond a few months at most. By lunchtime, Sophia had offered us a second-floor apartment, contingent upon the credit check. Shelly and I took turns shaking her hand, reasonably confident that nothing would prevent us from moving to this nicer, calmer home. This retro apartment building would be our L.A. home for the next two years.

Before long, we were settled into our new place with our two cats, a female Persian we'd adopted in Japan and a male Tabby we'd found wandering the streets of Bucharest. They couldn't have been more different. Fujiko, our Japanese cat, was lovely and standoffish, while the Romanian orange-and-white cat named Harpo was as friendly as could be to nearly everyone. He quickly grew accustomed to his role as our cultural ambassador. No matter who came by, he'd welcome them by hopping into their laps or, at the very least, by rubbing against their legs as his traditional greeting ritual.

Both cats were well traveled by then. Fujiko had adapted successfully to four different countries: Japan, Thailand, Romania, and the U.S.

Harpo was destined to live in three. Shelly and I had discovered that traveling internationally with cats was easier than with dogs. They were smaller and their carrying cases fit under the seats of most aircraft. We could pull out a small bowl and fill it with water when needed at airport transit points. We did the same with a small litter box and a hand-sized portion of litter or crumpled paper for an instant toilet. Their requisite health certificates and proofs of three-in-one vaccinations were relatively easy to procure in the final week before travel.

With our critical logistical tasks accomplished, we started to investigate the quality of life in Los Angeles. What we saw and felt was most definitely to our liking. The Bucharest weather the prior two years was characterized by a steep drop in temperatures and a persistent shroud of heavy cloud cover, but L.A.'s fall weather couldn't have been nicer. One marvelous sunny day followed another. We even began to wonder if L.A. ever had to deal with winter. The fair weather persisted even after the holidays had come and gone. What finally qualified as a sort of winter that year, with the occasional cloudy or drizzly day, arrived around February and lasted a month or so before the balmy days started in again. We were adjusting our lifestyle and dress to this seemingly endless sunshine, adapting also the informality of speech and garb for which Angelinos are deservedly famous.

Our first year back was a very special time for relishing outdoor activities in this near-perfect climate. We became regular visitors to Santa Monica and Venice Beach, especially on Fridays after work. Shelly enjoyed strolling along the beach from Venice Boulevard towards the Santa Monica Pier. She also regularly attended a ballet class at a popular Santa Monica dance studio. I became an avid cyclist and inline skater, gliding along the sidewalks that seemed to go on forever, with one magical beach view after another. When feeling energetic, I tried to make it all the way from Venice Beach to Sunset Boulevard near Malibu and back. That constituted a good workout, especially after the long hours in the office and classroom.

We explored many good Westside restaurants. Our early dining favorites were the classics, establishments that had stood the test of time to become L.A. institutions. These included Canter's Deli in the Fairfax district, which was just a short drive from our new home, and Mel's Diner just up Highland Avenue at Sunset Boulevard. Both offered massive portions of the best comfort food around, such as deli sandwiches, stuffed cabbage, and blintzes at Canter's and oversized sandwiches, French fries and fountain drinks at Mel's. Who could ask for more?

We felt very young and active, although we were both in our forties by then, thanks to our brains being constantly challenged by our graduate coursework and stimulating new lifestyle. We escaped serious damage to our waistlines from this calorie-laden orgy by staying active. Of course, our self-indulgence could last only so long. During our time in L.A., our food preferences gradually evolved towards the much healthier California cuisine that would ensure us better health and more energy. In the early days, however, it was so easy to slip back into our binge mentality when the pressure of research papers and examinations intensified.

A highlight of our second term at USC was a course entitled Non-formal Education in the Developing World, again taught by Dr. Stromquist. Until then, I'd never distinguished between the formal schooling that takes place every day in bricks-and-mortar school buildings and the non-structured types of learning that occur in libraries, adult education centers, churches, and even in people's homes. Now we would learn to assess them in different ways. Non-formal Education (NFE) has been defined as educational programs that impart adult literacy, basic education for out-of-school children, life skills, and work skills. NFE programs don't necessarily follow the ladder system of traditional schooling. They may have a differing duration than school schedules and might or might not confer certification of the learning achieved.[46] From a broader perspective, they are intended to provide overlooked or marginalized populations with access to organized learning opportunities that reinforce their self-esteem, improve their life opportunities, and assist them to better contribute to their local communities.

Shelly and I could directly relate to many of the concepts and objectives of this course. We'd been tutoring with NAI and a few years earlier had collaborated with U.S. Peace Corps volunteers in Thailand. We knew that non-formal education programs were serving an important function, both in our own neighborhood and worldwide. In our class, we read and watched inspiring videos about the successes of NGOs around the world that were constructing alternative education systems for underserved populations, with a remarkable degree of success.

One of the most successful such organizations at the time was the Bangladesh Rural Advancement Committee (BRAC), whose mission was to provide non-formal primary education to those who had been overlooked by the formal system. These were generally poor, rural, or disadvantaged children and adult dropouts. BRAC schools typically consisted of just one room with one teacher and no more than thirty-three students. Core subjects included mathematics, social studies and English. The schools also fed the students and allowed for flexible learning hours, while providing scholarships based on good academic performance.[47]

It was refreshing to learn about ways motivated individuals working with their peers at the grassroots level could empower local communities and, eventually, entire countries through untiring efforts. Besides Bangladesh, India, Turkey, Pakistan, Afghanistan, and Thailand had benefited significantly from extensive networks of non-formal schools offering literacy, life skills, and, most importantly, hope to their students.

A key project for this class was to identify and construct a portrait of an NFE provider in the Los Angeles metropolitan area that was serving a marginalized population. We finally identified the Thai Community Development Center (Thai CDC), a relatively new non-profit organization established by Thai-American Chanchanit (Chancee) Martorell. She had gained considerable attention a few years earlier for her role in assisting a group of Thai garment workers who had been released from captivity in a notorious human trafficking case in El Monte, California.

That case had garnered international media coverage. Chancee's organization had acted as the service provider and advocate for the seventy-two Thai adults freed from a sweatshop during the raid by U.S. government officials. They had been held in dire conditions against their wishes. Chancee explained that she had been inspired by that experience to create the anti-human trafficking program and to use Thai CDC as a venue for offering a full range of social, legal, human and case management services needed by Thai trafficking victims. Thai CDC was already providing other critical services to low-income Thai immigrants such as legal aid, parenting classes, low-cost housing, small business counseling, and English-language literacy courses. While our class project profiled all these outreach programs, Shelly and I paid special attention to the adult literacy courses. We were so attracted to this effort that we soon became directly involved as volunteer instructors.

At the time, Thai CDC was offering English language classes to Thai adults every Saturday and Sunday afternoon. They studied on weekends because many worked long hours during the week and on Saturday mornings, too, mostly at service jobs as masseuses, waiters and waitresses, construction workers, day laborers, and shop clerks. Most of their employers were in East Hollywood, the traditional gateway for Thai immigrants to the United States.

This neighborhood, where Thais felt most at home, was bordered from west to east by Western and Normandie avenues, and from north to south by Hollywood and Sunset boulevards. As a result of a campaign organized by Thai CDC, the L.A. City Council would soon designate it Thai Town, the first of this kind of geographic entity in the U.S.[48] This designation was part of Thai CDC's economic strategy to revitalize an otherwise depressed and neglected section of Hollywood through cultural tourism.[49] Beyond that, it also enhanced the civic pride felt by recent Thai arrivals, those of legal and those of undocumented status.

Thai Town was one of a host of ethnic enclaves that came to define modern Los Angeles in a way that was unique among American metropolises. The older 20th-century L.A. enclaves such as Chinatown, Historic Filipino town, Little Tokyo, and Koreatown were located close to downtown L.A. These were joined by newer cultural districts farther afield in the city and in other parts of Los Angeles and Orange counties: Little Armenia, Little Ethiopia, Little Persia, Little India, Little Bangladesh, Cambodia Town, and Little Saigon. These specially designated neighborhoods strongly affirmed the diverse nature of Southern California.

Statistics demonstrate what a truly multi-cultural city Los Angeles had become at the turn of the 21st century. Outside of their respective countries, Los Angeles hosted the largest populations of Cambodians, Iranians, Armenians, Belizeans, Bulgarians, Ethiopians, Filipinos, Guatemalans, Hungarians, Koreans, Israelis, Mexicans, Salvadorans, Thais, and Pacific Islanders. It was home to the largest population of Japanese living in the United States and has one of the largest Native American populations in the country. The L.A. metropolitan area was also home to the second-largest concentration of people of Jewish descent in the Americas, after New York City.[50]

———•———

Our evaluation of Thai CDC's literacy program revealed a pressing need for trained English-as-a-Second-Language (ESL) instructors, who were needed to improve the quality of instruction for motivated immigrant students and to construct a sustainable curriculum. In reviewing things, we noted that there was only one regular instructor, a part Puerto Rican American and part Thai American named Ernesto who was a recent graduate of UCLA's Urban Planning program. Ernesto was using a very mainstream ESL textbook intended for beginner-level students with little to no prior exposure to English. Like many introductory textbooks, this one divided each learning unit into sections for English grammar, vocabulary building, and practicing real-life dialogues through instructor modeling and student repetition. This approach reminded me of my high school French experience. It seemed to us overly academic, considering the students' urgent needs to communicate in everyday contexts with Americans.

By closely observing several classes, we noted that several of the students had already acquired survival English skills from having worked in Los Angeles. They could talk about their work and life experiences, while admittedly making some grammatical errors that didn't prevent us from understanding what they wanted to say. This indicated they had already achieved a certain level of competence in communicating with native speakers—namely, Ernesto and us. This reminded Shelly and me of many Peace Corps volunteers we'd known in Thailand who had managed to communicate with their on-site Thai colleagues without necessarily achieving perfect accuracy in Thai. Our prior language-learning experiences were now informing our efforts to understand what might work best for a non-formal learning program.

The program lacked instructors and appropriate materials, which is all too common in non-formal learning environments where students have pressing real-life responsibilities that can distract them from their studies. Well-meaning program volunteers, while trying to do the best they can to serve a needy population, often don't achieve the results they could if they were better prepared or had better resources. For start-up non-profit organizations surviving on limited-term or unpredictable funding from private philanthropists, this is especially true. Thai CDC's employees in those early years were doing double, or even triple, duty to stretch the organization's budget as far as possible. For instance, Ernesto was also lobbying city officials and local merchants to recognize Thai Town as a separate entity in Los Angeles. Clearly his efforts paid off in that regard, but we could also see that the literacy program needed improvements that better trained volunteers might achieve.

We soon began leading the weekend literacy courses ourselves. This turned into a win-win situation for our students and ourselves. We acquired practical experience in adult ESL teaching. Our students benefited from studying with two instructors who had lived in Thailand, spoke some Thai, and were strongly interested in applying adult-oriented teaching methods that would enhance the quality and pace of their learning. We began by consolidating the two, weekend afternoon courses into one that took place on Sundays. From our observations of Ernesto's courses, it had been clear that the adult students who came to the Saturday class were frequently late, owing to work or family commitments. They seemed to lack energy after a hard week at work. By focusing on just the one afternoon, we made it clear to all that the new class would be relevant to their daily lives and worth the sacrifice of precious family time.

The course we created included several active learning components appropriate for adults; they were intended to keep students energized on their day off. For example, rather than just talking about American or Thai food while using a traditional textbook, we went out as a group to several budget-friendly nearby restaurants and modeled how to interact appropriately with waiters in English. We also discussed the meanings of different items on the menu. When we visited a local Thai restaurant, our students became especially animated and shared as much as their language abilities would allow. As we ate, we swapped stories of other restaurants and foods that we liked and could recommend, all the while bonding as a learning community. We also visited different local supermarkets, identifying fruits and vegetables in English and repeating the sounds several times to reinforce the new word in our students' minds.

This type of instruction, moving around as we did, is called the Total Physical Response (TPR) method and is defined as creating a brain link between speech and action to boost language and vocabulary learning.[51] It's been shown to be effective with students like ours who might have had short attention spans in traditional classroom environments. While using TPR, Shelly and I also decided that a task-oriented curriculum would work well with our migrant students' needs. In our learning activities, we tried to reflect and validate our adult students' real lives. In our classroom discussions, we zeroed in on the meaning of English words and phrases related to the tasks.[52] To determine what specific task-oriented props to include in our course reader, we talked informally with our students before and after our class. This served as a kind of needs assessment for constructing key language content for our course.

We responded directly to our students' input by including things that counted to them in daily life: forms related to housing and job applications, Internal Revenue Service tax forms, adult school application materials linked to their continuing education plans, and menus from our favorite restaurants. This volunteer work was turning out to be as rigorous as any paid training we'd offered previously for clients. Fortunately, the personal rewards of seeing recent immigrants gaining a firmer foothold on the rungs of American society were well worth the effort.

We were thrilled to receive job offers as instructors for USC's American Language Institute, starting the fall term of our second year at USC. We'd finally attained the jobs we'd been aspiring to since applying to USC's School of Education. These positions not only covered our tuition expenses, they also paid a reasonable monthly salary and provided us with extensive training in teaching academic English to international students. We ended up teaching at ALI for three years. The timing overlapped with our period of completing our required graduate course work, a term we spent preparing for and completing our qualifying examinations, and the nearly two years we spent researching and writing our dissertations. It was ideal employment, in that it complemented our academic pursuits and the semesters we taught at ALI were in sync with our own study programs.

In those days, Shelly and I fully expected to continue working in the field of education for the rest of our careers. There was steady demand for trained instructors of English-as-a-Foreign-Language (EFL) abroad and English as a Second Language (ESL) for learners in the U.S. Combined with our previous experience in teaching management and as corporate trainers, we felt confident that our repertoires as adult educators would lead us to rewarding and enduring careers. What happened in terms of our ensuing work ended up differently than what we once envisioned. While we did continue as educators for a few years more, we eventually moved on to do international development projects and, later still, diplomatic work.

Like many Americans, we were feeling hopeful at the turn of the 21st century. Higher education was still largely of the traditional, teacher-centered sort. Most university instructors in such fields as language teaching, the humanities, and the social sciences built their daily lesson plans around course workbooks, class handouts, blackboard diagrams, and lists that they would create while lecturing to their students. The norm for language class size was around fifteen to twenty students, and in other fields between twenty and thirty. Technology hadn't yet seized the central position in nearly all facets of education that it now holds.

Many of us still viewed technology as a way of supplementing hard-copy course materials. We sometimes wheeled in the audio-visual cart for visuals based on plastic transparencies displayed onto a large white projection screen or we showed short video clips intended to stimulate class discussions or check student understanding of key ideas. Tech support, as the name suggested, supported the main lesson content. The typical college classroom featured little technology and focused on people-to-people exchanges, which is precisely what drew Shelly and me to teaching and training in the first place.

We enjoyed getting to know our students as individuals. There were no such things as drop boxes for storing and distributing class documents, list-serves for sharing course information, online discussion threads for further exploring key class themes, or class platforms for conducting lessons digitally from off-site facilities. These learning technologies gradually became known in the early years of the 2000s, at least for the non-science disciplines. In fact, many educators of that time would have considered such tools as pie-in-the sky imaginings more appropriate for science fiction than as viable teaching instruments for real-life learners. How fast things would change and shake up these traditional, complacent mindsets!

Bearing in mind that this setting took place in the late 1990s, we can better appreciate the sort of training new instructors received upon entering the faculty at ALI. One key aspect that made a great deal of sense to Shelly and me, was for new instructors to be mentored by more experienced instructors during our orientation and the early weeks of teaching. Both of us shadowed our assigned mentors, meaning we sat in on their interviews with new students, observed them as they planned their lessons, and watched them as they taught actual lessons. They, in turn, visited our classrooms regularly, to observe how well we were covering the required course content while also using the Academic English teaching methods we had been learning.

Another integral training method ALI used was carefully monitored practice teaching. We formed small groups of instructors and the new ones were given a certain amount of time to draft a lesson activity and then lead the group in it. Fortunately, ALI had already developed a selection of course readers from which we could select our practice activities. Those materials were based on its many years offering top-notch lessons to international students. We enjoyed observing and emulating our more senior instructors. We knew that soon enough we'd be expected to teach our international students, so it was helpful to have a clear picture of what to do ahead of time. Our students' admittance as fully matriculated students at USC would be contingent upon passing our courses. To achieve that, they'd need to demonstrate that they possessed a high enough level of oral and writing skills in English to function in a mainstream university classroom at USC.

We were naturally a bit shy at first around our more experienced teaching peers, never having taught Academic English in this type of environment. What English language teaching experience we possessed had been gained from our recent adult literacy classes at Thai CDC and from having earlier taught general EFL courses at private English language schools in Tokyo. The stakes at ALI were much higher than they had been earlier. Our students' lives would be tangibly affected by how we assessed their classroom performance. We needed to stay focused on improving their English-language capabilities in measurable ways, to ensure their advancement to their intended graduate school programs.

We understood from the orientation materials and instructions that ALI students would be assigned to beginner, intermediate, or advanced

English writing and speaking courses. Their placements would depend on how well they performed on an essay assignment and in a scripted oral interview with ALI instructors. At each of the ability levels, there were clearly defined learning objectives monitored closely in terms of student progress. For instance, for Oral Skills Level Three, an intermediate course that was always fully enrolled, our international students were told to make a short, extemporaneous speech the first day of class for us to assess their language strengths and weaknesses. As instructors, we could then tailor our lesson plans to help them conquer any weaknesses we'd observed. By providing consistent and caring hands-on coaching, we observed these students gradually acquire the skill sets needed for success. At Level Three, they worked through a progression of projects during the semester that included an informative presentation to their peers, followed by a compare-and-contrast speech to describe the pros and cons of a product or a policy, to a final student debate about a compelling current event.

We understood that one of our main roles was to model for our students the key aspects of any given project. For instance, for the informative speech assignment, our students needed to know how to choose an important topic, how to grab and keep their audience's attention, how to organize their theme into two or three main points, how to use evidence and examples to support these points, and how to end their talk with a strong conclusion. By the time they'd finished level three successfully, our students were ready to move on to level four, which was equivalent to advanced intermediate oral skills. The next term, they would be performing even more challenging projects, such as creating and presenting a persuasive speech and negotiating with their peers.

Most ALI students at USC hailed from Asia and were either already enrolled or would soon be attending courses in USC's engineering, science, and business graduate programs. Back then and even now, Asian students dominated in the hard sciences. They had been raised in learning environments that were passive in nature, with their teachers expecting them to listen to lectures and parrot back correct answers.

ALI's approach was to demand a radical change in behavior for them, which made many at first uncomfortable. We needed to emphasize and reinforce the concept of cultural context shifting[53], meaning that in the United States they'd behave a certain way in the classroom, but after returning to their home cultures, they'd shift back to the prevailing behaviors there.

As our students progressed through the different levels of English competence, they were acquiring the communication skills and the cultural mindsets of American graduate students—namely, a logical, organized, and self-motivated approach to learning that American professors expected from them. We were molding their personalities to some extent, to exhibit more American-style attitudes and behaviors that they could flip on or off according to whatever situation they encountered in Los Angeles. Having acquired this same mental dexterity when we were coping with Asian and European cultural contexts overseas, Shelly and I felt very fortunate to pay it forward with these students.

———————

After being at ALI for only a year, we completed all our required graduate coursework in the School of Education. We had even survived the incredible rigors of a course called Multivariate Regression Analysis (MVRA)—better known as Logarithms for Educators. I'm hard pressed now to explain many of the finer points of that course. I only dimly recall a nice, patient female instructor emphasizing over and over how important the Bell Curve was in doing any sort of large-scale population studies involving educational survey research. Any points too far removed from this Bell Curve, say of two variances or more, were considered statistically significant for research purposes. We were trained to concentrate on these data points.

For course assignments, we reviewed large data sets to determine such indicators as beta coefficients, Pearson coefficients, p test and t test results, and many more. My head aches remembering them all.

While we respected our more statistically astute instructor and fellow students, I knew from the start that Shelly and I wouldn't be among the geek contingent in the class. We did somehow manage to pass, through sheer determination and very judicious use of the sympathetic teaching assistant who advised us through nearly every project.

For two such non-quantitative researchers, the trauma of MVRA was lessened by a remarkably stimulating anthropology course we took the same semester. It focused on landmark ethnographic studies of exotic peoples, beginning with Bronislaw Malinowski's studies of primitive peoples in the Trobriand Islands of New Guinea. This was followed by a fascinating review of Margaret Mead's travels to Samoa and of her controversial studies of various native peoples in New Guinea with her husband, Gregory Bateson. Our professor for that course was Dr. Nancy Lutkehaus. She had once served as Margaret Mead's teaching assistant at Columbia University, which naturally impressed us.

The grainy black-and-white photos she showed us from late 19th and early 20th century field studies evoked the same thrill in us that those intrepid ethnographers must have felt while seeking new knowledge and enduring the isolation necessary for conducting field research in remote locations. We felt completely in our element in Nancy's class, which helped us a lot as we began to seriously consider what research topics we would select and where we would conduct our own field studies.

A highlight of this anthropology course was learning qualitative data collection methods: ethnographic interviewing, participant and program observations, community mapping, videotaping and video editing, and, most importantly, writing a case study. At its most basic, a case study is a method of exploring and analyzing the life of a social unit. Following this course, we decided to conduct our field research in northern Thailand. There we would put all these research techniques to good use. For that, we were indebted to Nancy and her inspiring class.

Shelly and I traveled to Thailand for two months during the summer of 2001, to search for viable field sites for our dissertation research phase. From our earlier experience while living in Thailand, and from our more recent work with Thai immigrants in L.A., we were convinced that Thailand possessed the right conditions for the advanced research we were planning. We had studied the country for years and had heard of its success since the 1980s in using a system of non-formal education for a variety of marginalized populations, including Hill Tribe people and migrant laborers. In building this system, Thailand had partnered with the U.S. Agency for International Development (USAID).[54]

With formal introductions from Thai professional acquaintances and friends, we were able to meet with the director of the Thai Non-Formal Education Department within the Thai Ministry of Education in Bangkok. He and his staff were kind enough to provide introductions to many non-formal education centers in the north of Thailand. For several weeks that summer, we drove around rainy and muddy Chiang Mai and Chiang Rai provinces, trying to determine which site or sites would work best for us. These programs and student populations needed to be compatible with my proposed research theme "Poverty, Community Education, and Empowerment" and Shelly's chosen theme "Gender, Trafficking, and Learning". Toward the end of our exploratory trip, we negotiated with directors of two Thai NFE Centers to do our field research at their sites. It was mutually agreed that we'd spend at least three months at our chosen sites the following summer and further, unspecified time after that.

Shelly's research site was located on the northern outskirts of Chiang Mai, where she would observe and assess a vocational training program for young Thai women who were considered at risk of being trafficked into sweatshop work or sex slavery. Her site offered them skills for income-generating activities that included sewing, hair styling, Thai massage, and retail shop management. The goal was to assist them in pursuing mainstream activities and resisting the lure of the allegedly more lucrative, but personally devastating, sex work.

My research site was a Buddhist temple in central Chiang Mai called *Wat Sri Suphan.* It offered vocational and high school equivalency training to low-income Thai residents, many of whom had recently been laid off from factory work and needed retraining in other job skills. This temple was one of several in the older parts of Chiang Mai that specialized in handicraft production. These handicrafts were distributed to popular tourist hotels and stores nearby. The temple was well known for its excellence in the production of silverware, silver works of art, and a variety of tourist trinkets made from silver. For my field research, I would observe and evaluate the intricate methods involved in their production. The silver-making process could be mastered through non-formal education instruction, and for some talented students it became an important income-generating activity.

———•———

Back in the L.A. area after that memorable summer, Shelly and I settled into a new home in Burbank, a medium-sized town near L.A. One reason we'd chosen Burbank was because even though Los Angeles is world-renowned for its traffic congestion, our normal commute to USC via the 5 and 110 freeways only took about a half-hour each way. We were driving to work one sunny Tuesday morning in September, discussing class-related matters while sipping caffeinated drinks. That term we were both teaching ALI's typical course load, which meant an oral skills class at 9:15 a.m., followed by an academic writing course at eleven o'clock.

As usual, the radio was playing at a low hum in the background, but the sound of our favorite smooth jazz station was mostly blocked out by our casual conversation. The music stopped suddenly, and a serious voice began making a prolonged announcement about some sort of crisis that was odd enough to interrupt our conversation. Turning up the volume, we were first puzzled, then stunned to hear the news that a jet aircraft had just plowed into the south tower of the World Trade Center in New York. The announcer was describing it as second hit, which of course meant there had been an earlier one, too. For a moment or two, we wondered if we were listening to an Orson Welles-type spoof. His famous 1938 "War of the Worlds" radio hoax [55] had panicked many people before the story was retracted. We told ourselves it just couldn't be true that an airliner had flown right into such a clearly visible structure in broad daylight!

It quickly dawned on us that the scenario of that day, September 11th, was far worse than any fictional program a radio producer could concoct. We listened to the gruesome, compelling details over and over, reports of overwhelming devastation characterized by fleeing and trapped office workers and heroic first-call responders rushing into burning buildings, which subsequently collapsed onto them and the streets of lower Manhattan. It was a truly mind-blowing incident for us, as it clearly was for our fellow commuters. The in-bound freeway traffic slowed to a crawl and finally to a complete stop, as drivers were attempting to process the unimaginable horrors occurring right then in New York City.

As if in a nightmare, we finally reached USC and parked in our usual parking spot on campus. We staggered from our car in a daze of disbelief and worry. Entering campus, we noticed faculty and students walking by in this same kind of stupor, some apparently not knowing where to head next. Desperately in need of normalcy of some kind, we reported to work at ALI. We suspected that at least some of our students wouldn't have heard the shocking news. Like other college students, many of ours typically studied late and awakened most mornings in a sleep-deprived haze. Many would be hurrying directly from their beds to class. We would no doubt have to convey the dreadful news to them and try to quell their fears as best we could. That is precisely what our supervisors at ALI advised us to do. There was no teaching in the normal sense that day. Rather, we met with our students and answered their questions as clearly and honestly as we could, with the limited information we possessed at that time.

Before classes started, we and other profoundly saddened and anxious colleagues watched television news reports replete with non-stop repetitive images of the Twin Towers burning and collapsing into mounds of rubble. The broadcasters were able to begin listing some names of the hundreds of victims of these terrorist acts, since it was close to noon in New York City. Our ALI classes were composed mainly of students from China, Korea, Japan, Taiwan, and India. In their home countries, media reports had already conjured up a portrait of our country as perilous and crime-ridden, riddled with potential minefields for unsuspecting international visitors. The events of 9/11 were only confirming every cultural prejudice our students and their families had already held about the lack of personal safety in the U.S.

We were still reeling from the shock when we entered our classrooms. We had agreed to try to put on our best professional faces and steel ourselves to respond to and even counsel any traumatized students. What our students expressed was predominantly shock and raw fear about what might happen in Los Angeles, considering the attacks in New York. Most of them had been awakened early that morning by jarring overseas phone calls from frantic parents back home. Since communication marvels such as Skype and What's App didn't exist then, they had to cope with overseas operators and the fuzzy background noise of international calls.

Our students' frightened parents had been watching the live news feeds from New York for hours, as they lived many time zones ahead of Los Angeles. Some had been pleading for their kids to get on the first plane back home, which of course would have been impossible during the air shutdown that ensued after the terror attacks. Others were urging their children to take cover immediately, meaning to find a fallout shelter and to hide out until the worst had passed.

I tried to assure these young adults that there was little possibility of a terrorist strike in our immediate vicinity. And I didn't know of any fallout shelters nearby. They didn't seem convinced at first. I tried to direct our discussion towards which buildings in Los Angeles they felt might be the possible targets of terrorist air attacks. None thought that the USC campus held any strategic value for terrorists. As L.A. had no obvious equivalent structures to New York's Twin Towers, the students eventually decided that different facilities would more likely be targeted, especially those that evoked American culture. We drafted a short list on the board: the Hollywood sign, Hollywood Boulevard, Disneyland, and Universal Studios. As none of those locales were close to campus, this discussion did help to diffuse their overall level of tension—to an extent.

Moving on, there seemed to be a clear need to consider why terrorists might be so mad at the U.S. that they would hijack several planes and fly them directly into such landmark American monuments as the Pentagon and the World Trade Center. This was a big challenge for all of us. I didn't feel ready to disclose too much about my political beliefs. As for my students, they had been culturally conditioned in their home countries to avoid highly inflammatory topics. It was difficult for them to be open in sensitive situations. Their educational training in the hard sciences had not prepared them for the deeply probing kind of critical analysis that such a question required. Most importantly, their intermediate level of English-language proficiency didn't provide them with the oral skills needed to speak abstractly on a philosophical issue of this kind.

What they eventually came up with were short but easily understood thoughts: The attackers were jealous of the American lifestyle, angry at Western values, and didn't like President Bush. At that moment, it seemed that even exceedingly difficult concepts could be stated simply after all. Nobody since has ever explained any better what might have been the motives for such gruesome attacks on that darkest day in American history.

———•———

Shelly and I went through the same stages of grief after 9/11 that most other Americans were experiencing. Denial of the act wasn't an option, considering the graphic images of people leaping from the towers and the incessant TV news loops reporting ever more tragic information in the days after the attacks. Yet, despite the clear evidence, somehow the attack methods and the scope of the disaster just didn't seem possible.

It was hard to fathom what kind of hatred would incite such heinous acts. The attackers represented a blight on humanity that would, unfortunately for all of us, progress even further in the years thereafter, as we heard reports of the rise of Al-Qaeda and the Islamic State in Iraq and Syria (ISIS).

Throughout that week of the attack, everyone—faculty colleagues, students, and us—were merely going through the motions of daily life, covering the minimum needed to maintain the façade of teaching and learning, but with little focus or measurable results. Finally, by the week's end, we all seemed to be progressing through the anger and depression stages together. When the final tally was reported—2,996 people killed, including 372 foreign nationals (12% of the total)[56]—It was hard not to rage at and despair over the fanaticism that led to their unjust demise.

We were still stuck in a dark mood on a rare cloudy day in Burbank the Saturday after 9/11. Our *Los Angeles Times* newspaper that morning was full of the latest revelations and stunned reactions to the tragedy. President Bush had flown to New York the previous day and made his now famous bullhorn speech to the gathered multitudes of New Yorkers. In it, he praised the firefighters' bravery for rushing into the burning buildings and he vowed to bring the evildoers to justice.[57] That certainly spoke to the anger that so many Americans were feeling, and it inspired millions of New Yorkers who were battered but unbroken by the unspeakable chaos and misery.

By late afternoon that day, we were both feeling restless, so we decided to head out on a drive with no special destination in mind. As we'd only recently moved to the San Fernando Valley, there were still many places to explore. At one point, we made a turn onto Ventura Boulevard, the main traffic artery through the Valley. What we saw simply amazed us. Red, white and blue streamers and banners were festooned on most of the street signs and traffic lights the full length of this boulevard. Ordinary Angelinos were standing several people deep on both sides of the street waving American flags and chanting, USA, USA! as New Yorkers had done earlier. For that weekend, at least, what united us as one American people and one strong, resilient, and unbowed American culture was on full display from coast to coast. It was impossible not to be moved and re-energized.

Despite the traumas of the national tragedy and the dramas of the graduate school qualifying examinations we were required to take that fall, Shelly and I somehow found time to do non-cerebral activities to maintain our sanity. One of the real benefits of living in a human-scale town such as Burbank was its access to community centers, which offered low-cost adult education courses to area residents. These courses ranged from the practical, such as "Starting Your Own Business", to the fanciful, such as line dancing and "Working with Mosaics".

We found introductory ceramics most therapeutic in terms of removing us from any sort of external mindset. We attended two evenings per week and preferred the build-your-own construction method to the throwing clay on the wheel one. The former allowed us to pound away at our clay to our hearts' content while shaping it into something recognizable. The creativity unleashed by doing things by hand or sometimes with the help of a plastic mold, contrasted sharply with the discipline and patience required when working at the pottery wheel. We craved this freedom of expression in our down time.

We must have constructed hundreds of pottery pieces. Shelly was the more prolific of the two of us. I'd started from scratch as a potter in our Burbank pottery studio, whereas Shelly was an intermediate potter or better, having studied in Tokyo. Her best pieces tended to be multi-textured bowls featuring a beautiful mix of luminous glazes. Our course instructors often praised Shelly's pieces for their originality. My production of misshapen plates and odd push pots more often invoked a puzzled silence from the instructors. Later, as I slowly got the hang of things, I produced some good pieces in my preferred glazes, either robin's egg or cobalt blue, which we proudly displayed in our home, alongside many of Shelly's master works.

A much more active alternative to pottery, but also therapeutic, was dancing, which we pursued whenever we could. Our two preferred activities were salsa dancing at the Boathouse at the Santa Monica Pier and swing dancing at the Derby in Los Felix. Both places were open to the public on Sundays for dancing. If we completed all our research commitments and household errands, we were ready for a break by then. The Boathouse opened at noon and continued well into the evening. The Derby opened at night and continued from eight o'clock until well past midnight. We appreciated the low-priced beginners dance classes that each locale offered when the doors opened, long before the show-off advanced hoofers started arriving.

This isn't to suggest that we were the awkward wallflowers some might associate with academic researchers. In truth, we both enjoyed getting out and showing our moves on the dance floor. Bear in mind that we had both come of age in the glittery disco era of the late 1970s. We could boast of our considerable prowess in doing the Electric Slide, the Hustle, or the Bus Stop, to name only three of that era's dance crazes. Shelly was the more accomplished dancer, having also done ballet and jazz dance for several years.

As both salsa and swing dance required the male partner to lead with a hand to the partner's back, for salsa, or with well-practiced arm movements for swing, it was my job to get up to speed on the basic rhythms of each. Fortunately, our instructors were very capable in maintaining the dance beat as they led us. Week in and week out at the Boathouse, our endlessly patient salsa instructor Alberto Torres reminded us beginner students that West Coast salsa always started with a pause. "Pause-two-three-four" he would exhort us throughout our routines.

We were mostly catching on. I started to love the physical sensations of spinning and dipping, and the crossing-over movements that I was leading. But, if I thought too hard about these mechanics, it was all too easy to have a dance floor collision with another novice couple, which could leave some painful bruises. Crushed toes were another hazard of salsa. Shelly was a good sport about my errant missteps onto her feet. Despite the minor risks, the many pleasures of salsa, not to mention the healthy aerobic workout, were well worth the effort.

An outing to the Derby frequently ended up as a kind of date night for us. We began with an early dinner at Louise's, the excellent Italian restaurant located adjacent to the Derby's dance floor, and then allowed ourselves enough time for proper digestion before moving on to our swing dance class. Although the beginner classes were always well attended and lively, just as they were at the Boathouse, the rules differed. We couldn't remain exclusively with one partner the entire class. Rather, participants had to rotate either to the left or the right, according to the instructor's orders. The idea was to try our new moves on a variety of dancers. Having a new and unpredictable partner each dance was intended to keep us all sharp.

Then the romance of our evening started to melt away, as our steady procession of new dance partners fluctuated from the standoffish (hard to lead) to the overly fresh (hard to fend off). At the end of class, Shelly would share with me who among her dance partners had possessed wayward hands and who were gentlemen. I'd share with her which of my partners had tried to lead me, who had sweaty palms, and who demonstrated real dancing talent.

By the end of most sessions, we finally succeeded in internalizing the catchy beat of swing dancing, thanks to the many repetitions of "one-two-rock step" we'd heard throughout the class. Swing, like salsa, turned into a rip-roaring workout over the course of an evening, forcing me to strip off one layer of clothing after another. By the end of the night, whatever clothing I still had on would be drenched in sweat. Any thoughts of a serious nature I might have started with would be long gone, too.

—·—

In the spring of 2002, we flew back to Bangkok, where we boarded our connecting flight to Chiang Mai for several months of field research. For those of you who haven't had the pleasure of trans-Pacific travel, such a trip serves as a potent reminder of the enormous size of our majestic Pacific Ocean. From our boarding time at LAX until our touchdown at our transit point in Taipei, our trip featured non-stop birds-eye views of the white ocean crests below for nearly twelve straight hours.

We spent our stopover at Chiang Kai Shek International Airport snacking on noodles and spring rolls and making a few purchases at the duty-free shop. There was also a very impressive national museum displaying beautiful artifacts in jade and cloisonné, as well as nice calligraphy brushwork and serene paintings and photographs of the fog-shrouded mountains and soaring birds of Taiwan.

From Taipei, we continued for another four hours before landing at Bangkok's Don Muang Airport, where we had to clear immigration and customs before walking over to the transit lounge to wait for our Chiang Mai-bound domestic flight. All told, the travel time was at least twenty-four hours until we'd arrived at our destination. The time difference between Chiang Mai and Los Angeles was fourteen hours; Chiang Mai was a day ahead. We departed on a late Friday evening from Los Angeles, and we arrived in Chiang Mai on a Sunday afternoon. Somehow, we lost Saturday in transit. Of course, we'd get it back later that summer, on our return trip to L.A.

At first, we were in no shape to do anything but rest and move slowly about as we tried to adjust to the time difference and the tropical heat and humidity of northern Thailand. We lingered for a while at our guest house, located in the historic center of the city. There we casually reviewed our study notes and the logistics for our upcoming research projects. Finally, feeling cooped up, we wandered through the nearby public market in Chiang Mai, which opens every Sunday afternoon and evening in the old city. Then we stopped to have a reviving drink and meal at our favorite restaurant, J.J. Bakery.

By the next day, we were sufficiently recovered to start making calls to our local Thai contacts. Most importantly, Shelly and I needed to reestablish contact with the directors at our research sites in Chiang Mai, the non-formal education centers we'd selected the previous summer. We were fortunate that both were available to meet us during our first week back. One important thing to always remember as a visiting researcher in another country is to bring gifts for your local contacts and research subjects. We had been sure to pack a small bag devoted to presents, including USC-brand t-shirts, notebooks, and fountain pens for our more important Thai counterparts and Hollywood tee-shirts, picture frames, and other touristy items for the local people we'd be encountering during our field research. As a visitor to another country, you step directly into other people's lives for an extended period, so you need to tread carefully and in a friendly way.

Another necessity for conducting academic research in Thailand was adequate language support, to ensure that we understood important conversations at our sites. While Shelly and I had long since mastered the finer points of "taxi cab Thai", there were more technical aspects of the language that we couldn't grasp, even then after several years' experience with Thailand and Thai culture. We recruited a small group of Thai-to-English interpreters and invited them to accompany us on days we were working at our sites. Our favorite interpreter was a former Peace Corps language and technical trainer named Nit, who had branched off into freelance work for the United Nations and other development organizations. She knew Thailand inside out and was a good friend from our earlier days with her.

Our other interpreters were graduate students from Chiang Mai University's English language department. Most did a good job, considering their youth. They knew their way around Chiang Mai. Our main challenge was to remind them to translate everything that was being said in interviews or informal conversations. They tended to filter out off-hand remarks by local participants that seemed irrelevant to them, but often proved instructive for researchers.

We enrolled in a Thai speaking class at nearby Payap University, on the eastern side of Chiang Mai. It took place every afternoon from one to four o'clock, with a small foreign student enrollment. This allowed us to ask our instructor about any new words or phrases we had failed to grasp on our morning's site visits. We also asked her to role-play planned interviews, to prepare ourselves.

By early June, we'd structured our weeks into a pattern. We conducted our onsite research in the mornings, accompanied by our interpreters, and we reserved the afternoon for Thai language courses. This structure largely defined our movements until the end of July. Of course, it was interrupted periodically as we pursued other research leads that took us further afield. Over the summer, Shelly expanded her research base to include two non-profit organizations, one in Chiang Mai and one in Chiang Rai, which were working directly with formerly trafficked Thai women. This took her away for overnight visits to Chiang Rai on occasion.

I also branched off from my main research site, to observe and evaluate a non-profit organization in Chiang Mai that was providing Thai-language courses to Burmese refugees, mostly construction workers living on the city's outskirts. This non-profit generally worked under cover of darkness, offering their courses in a private home after dinner, since many of their clients were working illegally in Thailand. The Thai government wouldn't have appreciated this, but the situation in neighboring Myanmar had deteriorated to such an extent that thousands of ethnic-minority families had no recourse but to seek shelter and work across the border.

Our final dissertations describe the field studies we conducted in northern Thailand from 2001 and 2002; these are available online in a more detailed and technical account.[58] They provide all the main sections that comprise a standard dissertation: the background explaining why we selected our research topics, our literature review of related studies, the methodology we used for our field research, the key findings that resulted from our studies, and the final recommendations we made based on these findings.

As this book is intended more for a general audience than for educational specialists, I'd like to steer your attention back to a few of the cross-cultural lessons we learned while doing our research project in northern Thailand. These may relate to actual challenges you face one day in working or studying in Thailand or in similar developing countries:

Buddhist influences are strong and enduring, and they are integrated into the lifestyles of most Thai adults.

A clear majority of Thais believe in the concepts of karma, rebirth, making merit, and the interlocking nature of everything. The Thai is certain his current situation is the result of accumulated actions, both good and evil, in former existences and the present. His actions are directed toward bettering his merit position, to achieve a better life now and in future existences.[59]

As we were actively intervening in the lives of local people of Buddhist beliefs, we needed to consider this mindset among the population we were observing. Rather than outsiders making suggestions for change, we needed to follow a cultural approach that allowed the community to take the steps necessary to transform itself in a self-reliant sort of way. Mutually aiding one another is an important shared value among community members in Thai society. A grassroots and communal problem-solving approach called *khit ben* had already been used in social development projects in Thailand for decades.[60]

Thais as individuals often have difficulty in expressing themselves and in being assertive.

They describe this characteristic with the word *krengchai*, which means deferring to those of higher authority than themselves. As outsiders with the accumulated resources of higher education and Western incomes, it was natural for local Thais to perceive us as having a higher status than they did. They adjusted their behaviors to be deferential towards us. We tried to minimize this as much as possible.

As sensitive researchers, we made every effort to dress according to local standards, wearing older Thai-style clothes, including loose cotton, wrap-around farmer pants and the typical blue cotton shirt or blouse of Thai workers. We ate with our research subjects and their trainers at their NFE sites as often as possible and spoke regularly to them about their families and communities, which they always seemed to enjoy and appreciate.

Thais generally don't appreciate open conflict; in their minds, social harmony must be preserved at all costs.

In fact, they take extraordinary measures to diffuse anger early on in a discussion. The *jai yen*, or "cool heart", is the ideal in Thai society.[61]

While working in a different language and culture and in the oppressive heat of northern Thailand, there were many occasions when we'd start to lose our tempers. Ideally, one of us would remind the other of the vital importance of public face and maintaining one's composure even in stressful situations. If things remained tense or frustrating, our next move would be to get away completely and return after a suitable cooling-off period. Figuring out how to maintain a cool heart in the steamy tropics is one of the many paradoxes of Thailand that continues to perplex the country's visitors.

——•——

We returned to USC in the fall term of 2002, replete with many notebooks of field notes, community maps, audiocassette tapes to be transcribed, and videocassette tapes to be analyzed from each of our research sites. Our challenge in the coming weeks was to plow through it all and make sense of it. Fortunately, our qualitative research course had taught us about the process of coding raw data, which is an effective way to manage research loads.

Coding is the process of sorting and then marking up research materials akin to what is done in preparing for a big household move. This was an activity that Shelly and I had experienced many times and had become quite adept at. Not surprisingly, we turned out to be good academic coders, too. We decided to color code our research notes and audio and video products into blue, red, and yellow categories. For the blues, we separated out materials relating to the educational methods of non-formal teaching and learning we had observed, including instructor coaching and mentoring of participating students. For the reds, we sorted out evaluations relating to the stated program objectives that had been described by site officials, versus the actual programming outcomes that we had observed. For the yellows, we zeroed in on those factors that we felt had affected participant learning and personal development in either a positive or a negative way. This type of methodical sorting helped us to manage a task that appeared overwhelming at the outset.

Having effectively organized our data, we then got down to work writing our dissertation drafts. It soon became clear that Shelly and I had strongly contrasting writing styles. I was normally more focused and energetic in the early morning and could crank out a page or two before leaving for work. On weekend mornings, my goal was generally to write three or four serviceable pages. Her approach was the mirror opposite of mine. Sitting down at her computer after we'd finished dinner and other obligations, Shelly wrote until midnight or later weeknights. She had the same rhythm on the weekends, but occasionally her writing would continue all night. On more than one occasion, I blearily sat down to work in the morning at my computer just as she was blearily signing off hers at the end of that night's work.

We felt fortunate to have very interesting material to work with, or this might have been a recipe for marital disaster. In my case, I was constructing a community profile and map of the neighborhoods surrounding Wat Sri Suphan. I was also reviewing and editing many hours of video I'd shot of the adult students at work, monitored closely by the Silver Master who served as their instructor. I also needed to transcribe nearly twenty audiotaped interviews with the program organizers and participants. Shelly was constructing a complex chart that would indicate what factors were most likely to lure young Thai women into being trafficked. She also did program evaluations of the three different providers of vocational training for at-risk Thai women she had observed, including her main Thai-government supported research site and two other Thai non-profit organizations.

We were intensely focused on making steady progress on our disser-tations and completing our USC doctoral degrees, but we also needed to continue working to support ourselves. Before we headed off to Thailand in May, our three-year contracts at ALI expired. The uni-versity would no longer support our tuition, but we were expected to continue paying for a certain number of credits each term as enrolled students. We made contact that year with a very dynamic Taiwanese woman who was herself a recent PhD graduate from USC's School of Policy, Planning, and Development. Dr. Joanna Yu had been hired as the marketing director for a new program called the International Public Policy and Management (IPPAM) program. This program was already quite successful in recruiting public officials from Indonesia and East Asia to come to USC for a thirteen-month-long executive master's degree program in public policy. Typically, a cohort of forty to forty-five students arrived in June of one year, and thanks to the magic of IPPAM's intensive curriculum, that same cohort would graduate the following July.

IPPAM was looking for American graduate students with prior expe-rience living and working in Asian cultures to serve as foreign student advisors and teaching assistants in certain courses. As Shelly and I were working on our own dissertation-related project evaluations at that time, we proved to be a good match. As a real plus for us, the IPPAM staff members fully understood how hard we were working on our dis-sertations and actively supported our research efforts, providing us with an invaluable degree of flexibility in our working hours.

The program had been founded a few years earlier with the help of a large grant the USC's Policy School received from the Indonesian government, to train a cadre of promising Indonesian public officials. IPPAM's first few cohorts had included a student base gleaned mainly from these officials, who took approved leaves of absence from their jobs in the Indonesian ministries. By the time we joined IPPAM, though, the number of Indonesian students enrolled in IPPAM was rapidly declin-ing, due to the U.S. government's clampdown on male students from

Muslim countries after the 9/11 attacks. While Indonesian females were still receiving student visas for higher education in the U.S., Indonesian males were not so fortunate.

Fortunately for IPPAM, Dr. Yu was able to replenish the IPPAM student numbers by recruiting a growing contingent of officials and private-sector students from China and Taiwan. Of course, the culture of IPPAM would have to adapt to the Confucian values of a stronger student cohort from China. From a largely Indonesian program, IPPAM was fast diversifying. Shelly and I noted that the Taiwanese and Chinese students came from quite different backgrounds. The Taiwanese, accustomed to democratic values and a booming economy, often had prior work experience in private-sector family businesses. Mainland Chinese, by way of contrast, were mostly officials from Chinese government ministries and thus had to toe the party line. Those Indonesian students who remained in the program were acculturated more in a Southeast Asian way, meaning they were clannish like most Asians, but also quick to laugh and generally more mild-mannered than those from certain other countries.

There could have been considerable tension within IPPAM, but this was largely non-existent. An important reason for this was the way the program was managed by Academic Director Dr. Joyce Mann and her able assistant, Ann. Dr. Mann was one of those rare individuals who could assess huge volumes of public policy data and reports while maintaining a wonderful sense of humor. She served as an excellent role model for how managers could be both competent and personable at the same time.

Both Dr. Mann and Dr. Yu believed that visiting groups of international students should enjoy an authentic American experience during their stay at USC. They turned to Shelly and me to serve as American holiday event coordinators on many occasions and praised our active participation. During our four years working with IPPAM, we celebrated American holidays with our students. We took them to Joanna's lovely home for a Fourth of July barbecue and fireworks each year.

At Halloween, Joyce and Ann decorated the program office in creepy décor and encouraged everyone to show up in costume. At Thanksgiving, all IPPAM students were invited to celebrate a potluck dinner that Joyce and the staff organized. This was true at Christmas as well – and no student went home without a present.

This familial approach resonated well with nearly all the IPPAM students, who were far from home for an extended period and often for the first time in their lives. Over the course of the year, the change in how they felt about themselves and about USC and American culture overall was striking. Whatever reticence or trepidation the students might have felt when they first arrived largely vanished by midyear. Many group outings helped to achieve this result. For instance, each year during our IPPAM tenure, we made trips to the L.A. Memorial Coliseum for USC Trojan football games, did walking tours of Hollywood or Santa Monica, and celebrated Chinese New Year over a banquet at Empress Pavilion in Chinatown, one of L.A.'s very best Chinese restaurants.

The most memorable IPPAM event ever for us was our group ski trip to Big Bear one year. We rented eight or ten cabins for use by our students and other participating staff members and carpooled to the resort from L.A. Mother Nature cooperated nicely, providing a scenic display of snowfall that started just after we all checked in that Friday evening. The next morning, everyone was eager to get to the slopes early, for their first-ever attempts at skiing. In fact, for most of our students, this was their first time to witness snowfall.

Naturally, some of the students and their families hadn't come equipped with the latest skiwear, so they bundled up in layer upon layer of clothing. Before any skiing, there were snowball fights to be had, snowmen to build, and many, many group photos to be taken for the folks back home. The process of taking photos involved bringing all our participants together for a kind of group validation of all the fun we were all having. In this case, the fun and laughter continued all the way to the ski slopes. Many of our novice skiers could barely remain upright, having never experienced an icy surface before. No matter, they just kept on trying to get up and eventually made it upright. After a mighty effort, they arrived at the top of the beginner slopes. Often, their all-too-quick downhill slide was one long tumble. Their laughter drowned out any yelps of pain from the many falls.

———————

By that spring term, Shelly and I were scheduled to defend our dissertation research and written manuscripts before our faculty advisory committees. It was very important to be prepared for any questions they might ask us. Our committees were composed of two faculty members from our home department in the School of Education and one professor from an outside program. My outside professor was based in USC's Sociology Department and Shelly's in the Anthropology Department.

The defense, as it was called, was reminiscent of a legal defense at a trial. The classroom where it was held was a formal one. When I walked in, the chair of my committee, Dr. Rideout, greeted me and told me to sit directly facing the three faculty evaluators. He began things by asking me to provide a brief overview of my research. Before long, each of them was taking a turn probing me about the significance of my study, my methodology, and my results.

By that point, I'd already spoken with each of them at length about all these themes and we'd ironed out most of the nagging issues. Having worked hard on my topic for eighteen months straight, I had gradually become one of the world's leading authorities on community education in Thailand. The same was true for Shelly at her defense. Over her study period, she mastered a whole host of issues related to the causes and effects of human trafficking of women in Thailand and could speak at length about any of them.

Even with all our accumulated expertise, however, we still encountered some unexpected challenges. Most university professors pride themselves on their keen intellects, and our committee members were no exceptions. During our defenses, Shelly and I were made to sweat a bit, especially in defending our final study results, which were based primarily on site-observations and extensive interviews, rather than on hard, empirical data. In quantitative studies, the researcher can always refer to the statistical indicators I noted earlier in this chapter when discussing significance. For qualitative researchers, as we were, there were none of these. We based most of our main findings on our keenly-honed perspectives from our months of observations and interviews at our sites, not to mention our overall competence as academic researchers. One method that proved a big success at our defenses was the video footage we'd shot at our sites. Both Shelly and I had spliced and edited hours of videotaped materials into roughly fifteen-minute feature films highlighting our experiences. On the screen, in full living color and with an accompanying soundtrack, our faculty advisors could get the full effect of our research projects. Their overall reaction was a positive one.

We passed our defenses. The rest of the term moved by in a kind of self-congratulatory swoon that lasted for weeks. In May, Shelly and I gathered with the other graduating students from USC's School of Education, including the hundreds who would be receiving their bachelor's degrees, the many who would receive their master's, and our smaller cohort that would be receiving doctorates in philosophy (PhDs) and education (EdDs).

All of us in this final group were positively glowing that May morning, both from the pride we felt as academics and from the strong Southern California sun. We marched down Trousdale Parkway on USC's campus in our scarlet robes, with our mortarboards and tassels and our dark blue sashes, surrounded by cheering families and friends gathered nearby. It was an amazing experience to be graduating once again, with all the pomp and ceremony, feeling absolutely as light as air that entire day.

After graduation, we still had months of editing before our final manuscripts were in publishable form. Still, the pressure of meeting one academic deadline after another was finally gone, and Shelly and I could release a collective exhale and begin focusing again on our everyday lives as Southern California residents. What this meant was finally having time to appreciate the "Big-C" cultural activities L.A. offered, and there were many.

At the top of our list of most favored places was the L.A. County Museum of Art (LACMA), which seemed to organize one spectacular exhibition after another. We stood in line with everyone else to gaze at King Tut and marvel at how well preserved the Egyptian antiquities were; they had survived so many earlier tours to museums all over the world. LACMA did many public outreach activities in those days. The museum was succeeding in bringing Angelinos together for their regular series of classic films, Friday afternoon jazz performances on the terrace, and their attractive café and gift shop. Stopping by LACMA was always a nice escape from whatever pressing tasks we were facing.

Another favorite of ours was the Huntington Library and Botanical Gardens in nearby San Marino. Its Japanese garden was as good as any we saw in Japan. We also attended a groundbreaking ceremony for their ambitious Chinese garden project. The Huntington Library Tea House, with its wonderful high tea and exceptional views of the ever-blooming rose garden, was an experience Shelly and I savored. A visit to the Huntington was as close to a trip to a well-endowed English estate as we were likely to find in the Los Angeles area.

For the next few years, we spent a lot of time in Burbank, only venturing overseas occasionally. Burbank had much to offer, with so many film studios headquartered there. It had successfully reshaped its main commercial street, which is called San Fernando Boulevard, into a very nice place for dining and shopping. At that time, it enjoyed a first-class theater group called the Colony Theater, which featured shows that often moved on to Broadway after their local run. Burbank was also special in having hillside parks that were just minutes away that offered the solace of unspoiled nature and challenging hiking trails.

We were enjoying the California dream life that had attracted millions of American seekers of the good life, although the trend in those days was outward from the State.[62] We could see the rationale for moving in either direction, as California still offered a stimulating and diverse lifestyle in America's arguably best climate. At the same time, we were deeply aware of the high cost of living, its burdensome tax system, and the frequent gridlock on its major freeways and on surface streets, too. California offered us a mixed bag, but to date we've never experienced a place that didn't.

We eventually transitioned out of our jobs at USC and began feeling the sort of restlessness we'd known on previous occasions. We took two extended trips, one to Vietnam, where a fellow Trojan graduate invited us to speak of our experiences to several local educational groups. We followed that up with a memorable vacation to England and Ireland, which included a stopover in my ancestral heartland in the south of that country.

As we stood on the banks of the River Lee in Cork, I tried to imagine my Great-Grandfather Frank Rynne many years earlier leaving his hometown and his Irish family behind forever at age fifteen, to head off alone on a lifelong adventure to America. He'd tried the previous year as a stowaway on board but had been caught and sent home. This time he borrowed his family's accumulated savings, which had been stashed in a coffee canister. With this he was able to purchase a lower- deck ticket on his second attempt and finally headed out to sea.

I could relate to the wanderlust he surly felt, as I had felt something similar on many occasions in my own life. I knew also that his motives had been linked to the desperation that characterized life in Ireland for much of the 19th century. Back then, British landowners in Ireland had shown an unimaginable degree of greed and oppression towards the Irish, and that directly led to at least two tragic and largely avoidable potato famines. The alternatives for legions of impoverished Irish were either a perilous flight to the New World over rough North Atlantic waters or staying home to face starvation, which happened to one million Irish nationals. An estimated five million Irish immigrated to the United States throughout the 19th century, more than half of Ireland's population at the time.[63]

Frank's departure from the port at Cork had taken place 130 years before our visit. Over the course of four generations in America, his six daughters, seven grandchildren, and twenty-six great grandchildren, including me, have all become loyal citizens of a wildly diverse and special country. We are the tangible, living results of his American dream and have served as a vivid example of the great American experiment in welcoming the world's dispossessed. Without that welcome and the subsequent freedom that Frank was granted to begin a new life on the bottom rung of U.S. society, none of our stories would have been possible.

After returning from that special trip to Ireland, Shelly and I were soon preparing for new overseas assignments in the Asia-Pacific region. Our life in Southern California would be ending, at least for a while. The downside to regular moves abroad was having to say goodbye to loved ones, and not necessarily knowing for how long. Our upcoming journey would take us back to the Asia-Pacific region we enjoyed and knew well. This next phase of our nomadic life would involve our participation in several international development projects in far-flung locations. The largest and lengthiest of these was my stint as country coordinator for a U.S. government-sponsored educational exchange program in Jakarta, Indonesia. The varied cultural lessons we learned from living in Indonesia, the world's largest Muslim-populated country, came next.

5: Jakarta, Indonesia

Sekali merengkuh dayung, dua tiga pulau terlampaui!— An Indonesian Proverb
(Do multiple tasks at one go!)

Jakarta offered a colorful palette of cultures, which seemed appropriate, considering our earlier focus on diverse populations in developing world contexts. The capital of Indonesia is a complex, but friendly, city that rivals Los Angeles for its size and head-spinning array of ethnic groups. For the international visitor, this translates into countless daily opportunities for cultural insights. But Jakarta is first and foremost a challenge, with its jumbo-scale office towers and shopping malls, non-stop buzzing street life, and thick religious overlay of Muslim, Christian, and Buddhist elements, which affect daily life in profound ways. The very fact that nearly 30 million people[64] live and work in metropolitan Jakarta on the narrow, northwestern coast of Java is little short of miraculous.

Travel from the United States to Jakarta involves an epic journey. During the two years we lived there during the late 2000s, our trips to and from Indonesia were as rigorous as any we ever undertook. From Los Angeles to Jakarta normally took around twenty-four hours, including long layovers along the way in Taiwan, Hong Kong, or Australia. Arrival times in Jakarta for incoming international flights were frequently in the dead of night, so it was rare that a friend or colleague would wait there to welcome us in the Arrivals terminal.

Shelly and I made our first trip to Jakarta just a few days before my Indonesia-based project was scheduled to start. We landed at the Sukarno-Hatta International Airport one early, early August morning. Our Qantas flight from Sydney had been scheduled to arrive the previous evening but had experienced engine trouble somewhere over Australia's far northern territory and had been told to return to its point of origin. After we changed aircrafts back in Sydney, the Australian authorities allowed us once more to depart for Indonesia. It was very surreal to re-do most of the same flight the same long evening. It was past two o'clock in the morning when our flight finally touched down safely. Naturally everyone on board cheered with relief.

Our first impression of the city was of a sleeping metropolis, temporarily quiet but sure to stir before long. We hoped to be safely asleep in our new apartment by then. At that wee hour of the morning, only a few bleary-eyed Indonesian family-members had come to meet other passengers from our flight. Everyone was still chattering about the unexpected turn-back and how unnerving it had all been. Amidst all that, I looked around and noticed a few squatters snoozing on the floor near the baggage carousels. The airport was about as desolate as it could be, with the fluorescent lighting set at low voltage. We waited for what felt like an eternity before our luggage finally appeared.

When our assorted bags turned up, we looked around for an airport porter. Not yet knowing more than a few words of the local language, Bahasa Indonesia, we relied on the universal language of waving and looking beleaguered to lure an older man towards us. *Trimakasi* ("thanks"), we repeatedly said to him as he strained to lift each bag onto his trolley. We had four large suitcases and two tightly packed boxes of teaching materials for him to move from the conveyor belt to our airport transport vehicle.

In Indonesia, I served as a coordinator for a U.S. State Department-sponsored project called the English Language Fellows (ELF) program, and that required a lot of textbooks and supplies. I brought whatever I thought might be immediately usable and sent the rest through the U.S. Embassy's Armed Forces Post Office (APO) mail system. Those packages arrived a few weeks after we did.

Even in the pre-dawn hours of our first morning there, many taxis idled outside the terminal as we exited through the automatic doors. The taxi service that an Indonesian friend had recommended was called Silver Bird, and it came equipped with an English-speaking driver and Mercedes Benz-style vehicle to whisk us away to downtown Jakarta and our new apartment. This type of transit came at a relatively steep price, but for the comfort of its cool leather seats, spacious legroom, and cranked-up air-conditioning, we were glad to pay whatever the fare might be. As we hadn't yet gotten used to the Indonesian rupiah/U.S. dollar exchange rate, it was hard to gauge what amount we were paying the driver.

We knew that cheaper fares were available from competing taxi companies, such as Blue Bird and Gamya, and we would later use those firms regularly. However, the seating and luggage space they provided in their smaller sedans were better suited for times when we were less burdened. And besides, after two long flights from Australia, we desperately needed some T.L.C. We finally collapsed into our deluxe transport and sped out onto the Jakarta Airport Highway.

————•————

My decision to accept this new project had been a leap of faith, in the sense that neither Shelly nor I had acquired much knowledge of Indonesia up to that point. What we knew had been gleaned from conversations with the Indonesian students we taught at USC. Many had by then returned to their government jobs in Indonesia with a USC executive master's degree in hand. Several would serve as our tour guides and cultural advisors during our residence in Jakarta.

A little of what we'd learned about Indonesia had also resulted from a short vacation to Bali during our Tokyo era, in the late 1980s. That trip had been a truly marvelous interlude but provided no real preview of Jakarta. Bali is an anomaly in Indonesia in that it has preserved its Hindu culture for hundreds of years in a sort of splendid isolation. Its world-renowned artistic paradise is steeped in elaborate rituals that are uniquely its own. In many ways, Bali is a place unto itself, and many foreigners who visit find no reason to travel further afield in Indonesia.

The island is located east of the main Indonesian island of Java. Its well-deserved reputation for ethereal spirituality was badly damaged by a horrendous series of bombings that rocked its Kuta Beach, a tourist area, in October of 2002. More than two hundred people, mostly foreigners, were killed in the attacks. The group that claimed responsibility was later identified as Jemaah Islamiyah, which was linked to Al-Qaeda.[65]

Jakarta is the Indonesian capital city. Located in western Java, it is worlds away from Bali, having been profoundly shaped by four hundred years of Muslim pre-eminence. Islam seemed to be omnipresent in the city, from the plethora of minarets scattered throughout, to its halal foods available at public markets and food stands. Sadly, Jakarta was also the scene of several terrorist attacks in the 2000s, including two bombings at the American-owned J.W. Marriott Hotel and one at the Australian Embassy.[66] These targets were places where Westerners gathered, so many foreigners in those days approached large international gatherings with a sense of dread, never sure when the other shoe might drop. Even so, American officials, business people, and others who worked in Jakarta continued to remain loyal to American hotel chains for holiday parties, weddings, and other special events.

As I was getting ready to begin work on my Jakarta-based project, Shelly was preparing to return to a project of her own, in the far-off South Pacific. The U.S. Peace Corps had once again offered her an overseas position supervising programming and training for its American volunteers. She served in a similar capacity in Bangkok during the mid-1990s. By the time we arrived in Jakarta, she was already working in the small, but incredibly diverse, nation of Vanuatu, near Fiji. Vanuatu has a rich culture with a unique history that stretches back many centuries. It consists of a chain of sixty-six islands, and the chain extends like a string of pearls from far northwest, near the Solomon Islands, to its far southeast location, near New Caledonia.

Vanuatu's colonial era was a colorful one. In the 19th century, France and the United Kingdom both claimed parts of Vanuatu, and they eventually agreed upon what was called an Anglo-French condominium, to manage what were then called the New Hebrides islands. This arrangement lasted until the Republic of Vanuatu was proclaimed in 1980. Even as an independent nation, though, the population has continued to live under the dual cultural influences of the two former colonial powers. A small majority of the country identifies with its Anglo heritage and speaks a pidgin form of English called Bislama. A smaller, but still sizeable, population subscribes to French customs and speaks a Creole form of French.

Prior to moving to Indonesia, I spent several months in Vanuatu with Shelly. We had both been trained by local Peace Corps language staff to speak Bislama, and after several weeks of study, we were communicating reasonably well. While we relied on Pidgin English for daily communication during the time we stayed in Vanuatu, we could also understand the local brand of French. Pidgin and Creole languages are widely spoken on island nations around the world, including in parts of the South Pacific, the Indian Ocean, offshore Africa, and the Caribbean Sea. They have been described as a baby-speak approach to communication and are employed to get what you want quickly, using whatever terms of reference you can.[67] To give you a flavor of Bislama, here is how I might have greeted a Vanuatu friend, called a *Ni-Vanuatu*, upon meeting him: *Mi glad tumas a save ti.* It could be translated as, "I'm happy to know you."

Shelly was contractually obligated to stay on there for several more months. Vanuatu's capital city, Port Vila, was located about two days away from Jakarta, owing to the limited flight options available between Vanuatu and Indonesia. All possible itineraries required at least a night's stopover both ways, either in Sydney or Brisbane, Australia. While this wasn't exactly a hardship, considering how attractive both cities are, the time and costs involved made it prohibitive for more than the occasional visit.

This would be our longest period of separation, and we were dreading it. However, such working arrangements aren't uncommon for couples in positions involving international development. I haven't seen the divorce statistics for those in our chosen careers, but sad anecdotal evidence indicates that many couples drift apart and eventually divorce after enduring several long separations of this kind. At that juncture, we were resigned to gritting our teeth and being as stoic as humanly possible during what ended up being four months living apart. Despite the brave fronts we put up, though, we felt miserable apart. There was a palpable sense of relief when Shelly finally rejoined me in Jakarta that December.

On the morning of our arrival in Jakarta back in August, we gained access to our new apartment at four o'clock in the morning, with the assistance of the night doorman, who was on duty and awake even then. As in many developing world cities, most modern apartment buildings in Jakarta employed a fleet of security officers and other staff, as well as imposingly high walls, to discourage interlopers. Our high-rise compound in the Menteng section of town was no exception. It was highly fortified.

My immediate American predecessor in the position I was assuming had recommended me to her Indonesian landlord. This had made it possible for us to step right into a furnished apartment. However, Shelly and I hadn't seen more than a few snapshots of it prior to arriving, and those only offered glimpses of the kitchen, dining area, and balcony. Consider our reaction upon entering and encountering orange-speckled marble tiling on the floors throughout the apartment. It was as slick as ice. We took our shoes off and slid across our spacious apartment in a sort of befuddled haze, opening the two bedrooms' doors, to discover bright peppermint-colored bedspreads on the already made-up beds. These unmistakable symbols of new money were evident even through the smoky haze of our jet lag and culture shock. We were relieved to see that the small kitchen and lone bathroom appeared normal and seemed to be in basic working order. Before long, we both surrendered to a much-needed slumber enveloped in peppermint green.

My sponsor in Jakarta was the U.S. Embassy's Regional English Language Officer (RELO). He and his assistant were coordinating a hectic three-day orientation workshop for the American teaching fellows in my program, all of whom had just arrived, as we had. Most were staying at a nearby hotel in the relatively international Sarinah district of central Jakarta and would be heading out to their teaching sites in other Indonesian cities after our training.

As the senior American teaching fellow, I was assigned to a base at the University of Indonesia (U.I.), the country's oldest, and one of its best, public universities. I would be overseeing and advising the nine other Americans educators during the coming academic year. There would be plenty of in-country travel for me to Surabaya, Jogjakarta, and Makassar, for meetings with the fellows and their Indonesian counterparts. An important part of my job was serving as a cultural interlocutor, ironing out as best I could any problems related to the fellows' local working or living arrangements.

At the onset, though, we were just getting to know one another, as exchange program participants always do, and trying to imagine the challenges we would face in our classrooms while training Indonesian faculty and teaching English to university students. We also wondered how we would cope outside of work, how we would adapt to a culture that was, at least in part, anti-American. As so often happens in programs such as this, most of the participants were female, with just two other male participants and me in the group. This gender disparity was even more evident during my second year in Jakarta, when most of the fellows opted to renew, but others did not. That year, there were just two American men participating. Based on my own study and experiences, I've determined that young American men are less interested than American women in immersing themselves in other cultures. This is to their detriment, I believe, since a period of living abroad constitutes the best way possible to connect with our planetary friends and neighbors and discover our own values and resilience.

Daily life in Indonesia was infused with religious influences. This was noticeably different from most of our earlier travel destinations, except Thailand, where Buddhist chants and almsgiving rituals were visible every day. In most of Indonesia, Islam was omnipresent. I certainly expected to hear the loud muezzin's call to prayer for all adult males five times a day: before dawn, at noon, in the mid-afternoon, at sunset, and in the dark night. There is one mosque or another in nearly every corner of the city.

What I wasn't aware of as we arrived in Jakarta was that our first month in country would coincide with the holy month of Ramadan. This special time commemorates the period in which the Qur'an was revealed to Mohammed.[68] Most practicing Moslems are expected to fast during daylight hours. My Indonesian colleagues impressed me with their ability to continue whatever daily chores needed doing in the tropical heat while refraining from taking even a sip of water until the sun had set.

On a day-to-day basis, my activities were almost evenly divided between training faculty members within the foreign languages departments of U.I.'s two Jakarta-area campuses (one downtown, the other just outside of Jakarta in Depok) and coordinating the U.S. Embassy's teacher-exchange program, which had brought us all to the country. My reason for being at U.I. was explained well in the ELF program's goal: To enhance the overall English-teaching capacity overseas and to broaden foreign teachers' and students' perspectives on international and America-related issues.[69] This ambitious goal was frequently criticized as not offering measurable ways of determining how well we met it. We soon learned that we were really measured on how many teachers and students attended our courses and how well their test grades improved.

As the senior fellow in the largest program of its kind in the world, I was accorded the honor of mentoring the younger American teaching fellows. Being so large, the program also benefited from more funds available to it than in small countries. My direct supervisor at the U.S. Embassy had oversight authority, not only for Indonesia, but for several other countries in Asia. For this reason, I'd been deputized to keep an eye on far-flung Indonesia while he was away.

In my first meeting with my local university counterpart, Bu Sisilia (Bu is the Indonesian honorific for Ms., Mrs. or Miss) shared with me her hope that younger English language instructors in the English-language section of the foreign languages department could become more focused on improving the quality of their teaching. Bu Sisilia felt that by developing action research skills, we could help internationalize their teaching methods and the English language curriculum. This, in turn, would help to attract a larger number of international students to Jakarta.

She recognized that a performance-oriented approach might succeed, where the seniority system, so common in Indonesia and throughout Asia, was falling short. It seemed that those employees who stayed the longest at U.I. were benefiting the most in terms of their salaries, titles, and teaching loads. They weren't necessarily the best teachers. Consequently, a new performance evaluation system was being considered. What I'd already learned from working in several countries was that culturally-embedded attitudes and workplace practices are slow to change. Still, I was willing to do my part to try and advance the reform effort.

These objectives were directly in line with the goal of U.I.'s rector: to internationalize the university by offering up to fifty percent of all courses in English.[70] For that type of Westernization to occur, at least the younger faculty would need to become familiar with basic Western educational theories. I chose to begin with Dr. Benjamin Bloom's Taxonomy of Cognitive Domains and Dr. Howard Gardner's Theory of Multiple Intelligences in my teacher workshop series. Without a doubt, in doing so, I was imitating my Bucharest training methods, whereby I laid the foundation for new workplace mindsets among Romanian audiences by sharing leading management theories. This time around in Jakarta, I again felt that my twenty or twenty-five teacher trainees would gain valuable insight from these theories about how to better manage and motivate their English-language students.

I began this series in the traditional way, by using Power Point presentations that described the theories in a very methodical manner. In explaining Bloom, I emphasized that adult learners were capable of far more than just rote learning tasks. When properly taught, they could demonstrate higher-order thinking skills, such as processing information and critically analyzing their own learning needs.[71] Research has shown that motivated adults perceive tangible material or lifestyle benefits from the classroom activities they perform. Bloom also provided important insights about how learning involved not only mental discipline, but also emotional investment and even bodily movements, to ensure students' active engagement in the process.

A contrasting way of looking at student motivation, is developed in Gardner's Theory of Multiple Intelligences, which divides learner's strengths and weaknesses into certain innate abilities of the individual.[72] One learner might be proficient in music, while struggling mightily with math. Another could be great at making speeches in public, but falters on written reports. The language teacher's responsibility is to know individual learners and determine their unique learning talents. This student-centered ideology, which harks back to John Dewey's learner-center, public school approach[73], was strongly at odds with commonly accepted teaching practices in most Indonesian classrooms, where the focus was on teacher-centered instruction, with lecturing as a common method and scant attention paid to student needs or preferences. Under the new approach I was offering, teachers who relied overly much on traditional teaching methods, such as lectures and memorization activities that might have been suitable for the hard sciences or history, were diminishing the motivation of their language students.

After setting the context for our workshop objectives—namely, to break out of traditional teaching patterns—it was up to me to start modeling for my teacher trainees what I hoped they would be able to achieve. It's not unusual in many parts of the world, Southeast Asia included, that Western so-called experts are invited to share whatever knowledge and skills they possess, with a built-in assumption that somehow this will magically enlighten and improve the performance of their audience members. While I could feel this dynamic among my workshop trainees at first, I tried to deflect it, full well knowing that any deferential treatment I received wouldn't endure over the course of several months of real-life training. My goal was to inspire my Indonesian colleagues, not just to fill their brains with information and teaching techniques.

As a community of educators, we needed to create a lively and inclusive learning environment jointly, one that we would all enjoy. To foster a better understanding among us, I made a point of informally meeting with all my trainees. In no time, I learned that they preferred an active learning style in our workshops, so we could share real-world teaching experiences. This was a nice surprise, because a huge majority of classes in Indonesia are conducted in the teacher-as-expert format. These younger trainees were willing to try something radically different. While nearly all of them in their own English language classes were still being forced to focus primarily on grammar rules with their students, they were clearly hungering to learn how to incorporate practical communication skills, including everyday speaking and listening abilities, as well.

———

While I spent weekdays learning the ropes at U.I.'s foreign languages center in the high-density Salemba neighborhood, on weekends I made every effort to familiarize myself with the different parts of Jakarta close to my Menteng neighborhood. Many of the sites that Jakarta is most known for were within walking distance or just a short cab ride from my apartment. The MONAS national monument, for instance, the symbol of Indonesia's struggle for independence, was highly visible in Central Jakarta and located in the giant Merdeka Square. Its scale, and the size of things in Jakarta generally, was mammoth; simply walking within that central square consumed considerable time and energy in the city's steamy tropical environment.

I learned in a purely unplanned way that Jakarta's many elegant shopping centers offered air-conditioned respite from the heat, while also serving as pleasant places for power walking among many of the world's most exclusive shops. While Indonesia was, and still is, largely a poor country in aggregate, a sizeable slice of the urban population of Jakarta possessed the means to purchase high-end consumer goods. I was told several times that Indonesia was a large market for Mercedes Benz and BMW automobiles. Other well-known luxury brands, such as Louis Vuitton, Christian Dior, and Gucci, were also well represented at Jakarta shopping emporia.

I stumbled into Plaza Indonesia Shopping Center one afternoon early in my stay. Located in the heart of the city at Jalan (Street) M.H. Thamrin, it wasn't more than a ten-minute walk from home, and there always seemed to be interesting activities going on both outside (labor protests) and inside (cultural exhibits and fashion shows), along the highly polished corridors of this upscale mall. This was my haven of choice for several months. I especially appreciated the international bookstore that sold a few English language newspapers and offered a small selection of English language paperbacks, too.

Later, my preferred locale switched. Across the plaza sat the Grand Mall Indonesia, whose celebrated opening was held several months after we arrived in Jakarta. This mega-story retail complex had a Hard Rock Café, first-class cinemas, and several good international restaurants. I later discovered that conditions were equally nice at Plaza Senayan, a bit further south, which was known as an ideal family hangout on the weekends, thanks to its galleries for adults and play areas for kids. This became our favorite shopping outing our second year in Jakarta, by which time Shelly and I had moved our residence to the more suburban enclave of Kemang, in southern Jakarta.

The preponderance of these sheltered shopping environments convinced us that, for those who could afford it, these venues were serving as alternative realities away from the oppressive heat, noise, and gridlocked traffic of Jakarta's outdoor spaces. Of course, security was tight at all these upscale locations, and any visitors who didn't dress the part of affluent shoppers were unsubtly turned away. This reminded me of our experience when we were turned away at the Oriental Hotel in Bangkok years earlier. I had no doubt that if we hadn't been dressed in Western work garb, we could easily have met the same reception at these deluxe shopping centers. The rather shocking inequality of Indonesian society, though new to us, was pretty much accepted as a given among our Indonesian friends.

The cityscape of Jakarta suggested some sort of collectivistic and futuristic metropolis, replete with one huge commercial complex after another. Its principal traffic arteries, Jalan Jenderal Sudirman and Jalan H.R. Rasuna Said, served as sleek but ever-congested entryways into the commercial heart of the city. As my job required frequent travel between U.I.'s downtown campus in Salemba and its suburban one in Depok, I soon became aware of how much the city relies on these over-taxed roadways. I frequently had to traverse through Central and Southern Jakarta to exit the city and end up in bucolic Depok. Such a trip took anywhere from one to two hours by Blue Bird taxi.

While Jakarta does have a public bus system and antiquated rail network, these transit options don't necessarily serve the needs of the burgeoning middle and upper classes in the city who have their offices in Kuningan or Senaya. For them, private or for-hire cars are the main sources of daily transportation. For me, as well, there was no way I could wedge myself into a packed public bus, decipher the street signs as we moved jerkily along, and then transfer to two or three other buses before arriving near my intended destination. Such was the fate of the city's working class and poor. It was not an easy life for them.

Poverty was something we'd encountered in other developing countries besides Indonesia. The glue-sniffing subway denizens of Bucharest were among the saddest cases we saw in our earlier travels. In Jakarta, though, the effects of poverty seemed to be exponentially more tragic. We couldn't help but be appalled by the prevalence of very young street children begging on street corners and overhead walkways. It seemed to us as if some evil, Fagin-like uncle was passing through the streets of central Jakarta early each morning with a truckload of toddlers and stunted youngsters, depositing them in their designated spots. He must have given them strict instructions not to return before achieving a certain quota of handouts. The kids seemed impervious to risk; they were willing to run into traffic and rap on car windows to plead for money. Their success rate appeared to be quite low. Taxi drivers were immune to their appeals; most just waved them away.

I was using taxis for my daily commutes, and I quickly picked up enough Bahasa Indonesia to instruct the driver where I was going while he inched the taxi through Jakarta's mazelike roadways. *Jalan lurus* was an easy way to tell the driver to continue going straight. *Ke kiri* or *kanan* indicated left or right. Perhaps my most useful phrase was *bukan dengan cara ini* ("This is the wrong way").

Certainly, by my second year in Jakarta, I was frequently giving directions to my taxi drivers, many of whom had relocated from Central Java or points further east and were bewildered by the sprawling metropolis. Many Indonesians think of Jakarta the way that many Americans think of New York City, a place that is undoubtedly impressive and one to take pride in, but not truly representative of the rest of Indonesia. To see the real Indonesia, I needed to visit the Central Java cities of Sulu, Jogjakarta, and Semarang. Fortunately, all three were on my travel itinerary, since we placed American fellows at universities in each of them.

During my first few months in the country, I was scheduled to visit all the American teaching fellows at their scattered sites around Indonesia. As a prerequisite for participating in our program, their local university hosts had demonstrated that they possessed full-fledged English language programs that could use the services of a trained American educator. This also meant that nearly all our selected schools were in medium—or large-sized cities. I was soon reading everything I could about the locations I'd be visiting: Surabaya in East Java, Makassar in Sulawesi, Banda Aceh and Bengkulu in Sumatra, Banjarmasin in

Kalimantan, and the three Central Java locations mentioned previously. These sites were scattered all over this island country, which measures 2,644 miles in width and 688 miles in length.[74]

The RELO for whom I was working was an even more active traveler than I was. Michael was responsible for monitoring and promoting U.S. government-sponsored education projects from Japan through much of East and Southeast Asia. He referred me to his local travel agent, a savvy young Indonesian woman who spoke good English. For a while, she was making at least one weekly travel booking for me. While unable to describe all my site visits in this account, there are a few that follow that taught me important cross-cultural lessons that I continued to apply throughout my two years in Indonesia.

My first site visit in September took me to a small town less than an hour by car from Surabaya. Since the Jakarta-to-Surabaya air route was one of the most frequent ones in Indonesia, I was able to take the national carrier, Garuda Indonesia Airlines. Later, for site visits to places that weren't as popular in terms of traveler volume, I had no alternative but to take newer, private airlines that were just finding their wings, so to speak. The gradual move away from state-directed enterprises to privatized ones was a bumpy transition for Indonesia, and for its aviation industry especially.

In the first decade of the 21st century, Indonesian airlines experienced a long string of terrible accidents due to hard landings, improper retracting of aircraft slats, and overrunning runways. Most were caused by pilot error, and none of the major airlines was spared. Part of the trouble was due to the growing pains associated with several upstart airlines, such as Lion Air, Adam Air, and Sriwijaya Air, all of which were jockeying to give Garuda Indonesia some real competition.

Another related factor was that Indonesia is an equatorial country regularly beset by ferocious storms during its lengthy rainy season, from October to April. Pilots are often caught off guard when previously calm skies quickly turn menacing. I soon learned that late afternoon and evening flights were the most likely flights to end up either flying through the eye of a thunderstorm or being delayed while airports waited out a heavy deluge. The best flight strategy was to take the early morning planes, either departing from Jakarta or when returning, since nearly all destinations within Indonesia could be reached before noon. The early flights occurred well before the afternoon cloudbursts that occurred almost daily, temporarily relieving the intense tropical heat and humidity that invariably built up.

The upshot of all this turbulence in the aviation industry was that by 2007, international aviation boards had banned all Indonesian airlines from entering both the United State and the European Union[75]. This ban would remain in effect for many years. My first year in Jakarta was destined to be my "Year of Living Dangerously." It wasn't so much related to political uprisings, such as those of the Sukarno era that were dramatized in the popular Mel Gibson/Sigourney Weaver film of 1982[76]. Rather, my year was marked by the social upheavals caused by real and imagined terrorist threats and the country's over-stretched infrastructure. I ended up taking nearly every airline that was operating in Indonesia, not completely aware then of their lax safety records.

For my site visits, air travel was the only viable option, considering the mountainous terrain within Java and the Java Sea, which separates many of the main islands I would be visiting from Jakarta. Garuda Indonesia dominated travel to the largest cities, such as Denpasar (Bali), Jogjakarta, Surabaya, Makassar, and Medan. Regional airlines picked up the slack for medium-sized cities. I flew Sriwijaya Air to Sumatra and Lion Air to Kalimantan and Sulawesi. Both were no-frills operations at the time; travelers boarded from the tarmac and passenger legroom was at a bare minimum. On several occasions, I noticed that I was the only Caucasian on the flight. It strongly suggested to me that although a few well-known destinations in the country attracted millions of international tourists, much of the country was an undiscovered backwater.

Among these upstart airlines, providing onboard food wasn't a consideration. Scheduled departure and arrival times served as rough estimates rather than reliable guideposts, as flight maintenance and logistics were notoriously unpredictable. This often made it necessary for me to postpone or even cancel previously arranged meetings with local

counterparts at our university sites. Of course, Indonesians were culturally conditioned to expect this as a natural by-product of Indonesia's
jam karet ("rubber time").

For our American teaching fellows, this flexible approach to time
meant rethinking the whole Western concept of time management
within their classrooms and offices. As Jonna, our fellow in rural
Sulawesi, described it, she often had classes that were fifty minutes
long and some of her students were forty-five minutes late! How could
a teacher make reliable plans in those conditions? Another fellow,
Andrea in Kalimantan, echoed this same sentiment. Some days, rain
pounded down on the metal roof of the classroom. She knew that when
it was raining like that, many students would be late because they'd be
waiting some place on their motorbikes, she hoped under an overhang.
Mother Nature often trumped any plans that humans might have made,
especially during the long rainy season.

———•———

An important part of my project responsibilities was to ensure that our
fellows settled in smoothly at their sites up country. Early on, I received
worried emails from some of them, complaining about their lodgings,
host counterparts, or proposed teaching schedules. I was eager to visit
all of them early on but considering the challenges of traveling nearly
the length of the country, I had to draw up a plan to visit each of them
over the next few months.

I headed off for my first visit in mid-September, just weeks after
our program orientation in Jakarta. While visiting a public university
in a small town not far from Surabaya, I learned an important lesson
right away. Don't plan an official visit for the middle of Ramadan, the
country's annual month of fasting. Without intending it, I created an
untenable situation for my local hosts. Our American teaching fellow
Ellen and her Indonesian counterpart Bu Dian, the English department
secretary, met me at the airport in Surabaya and drove me around the

small town of Gresik, pointing out local highlights, such as the cement factory where many local families were employed.

We stopped into one of Ellen's English classes, where I observed her teaching a group of aspiring elementary school teachers. The class was moving slowly. Ellen and the students introduced themselves, sharing where they hailed from, the size of their families, and any hobbies they enjoyed. During the discussion, what really caught the students' attention was a necklace Ellen was wearing. Her students weren't shy about asking what it cost, what it was made of, and how serious she was about this man who gave it to her. This was an early example of how Indonesians ask probing questions of newcomers, especially foreigners. It was hard for them to understand the concept of personal privacy, even in a public forum such as this.

It was well past lunchtime when class ended, but we didn't go to eat as nobody else was eating or drinking. The school canteen was shuttered, as well. At least Ellen had brought some snacks that she managed to keep hidden in her handbag. She kindly shared some with me. Otherwise, I certainly would have gone hungry after a long morning that started in Jakarta. We nibbled as discreetly as possible on potato chips and fruit, not wanting to attract the attention of the local faculty and students, and we apologized to Bu Dian for eating in front of her. She reassured us, claiming that she wasn't even hungry and didn't expect us to keep the fast anyway. We weren't so sure, though, and felt rather boorish for disturbing the cultural expectations during Ramadan.

During those two days that I was there at the site, I didn't meet with the head of the English department or the dean of the School of Education. They were unavailable. This was the only example among all the site visits I would make over the next two years when I didn't meet with any high-ranking Indonesian university officials. Thereafter, it became a standard protocol on my visits that immediately after arriving at a university office, I'd be offered tea and snacks as a welcoming ritual. I then met with a department chair, who eventually escorted me over to meet a higher-level dean. During Ramadan, though, everybody was keeping a low profile, resting and doing the minimum work necessary during their dawn-to-dusk fasts. Classes and administrative activities were going on, but no one was expected to perform at a normal pace or to achieve anything more than routine results.

On this first of many site visits, I did get to see the house where Ellen was staying with a local family. She was enjoying the treatment they accorded her as a kind of older sister to the family's much younger children, although it left her with little time to herself. Again, the notion of personal space or privacy was an unfamiliar one to them. Like a lot of home-stay participants, Ellen had already been asked to tutor the children in English, and it was hard for her to say no to her host parents. How could she when her very shelter depended on them? I learned from this experience that a site visit during Ramadan was awkward, hunger-inducing, and culturally insensitive on my part. This *faux-pas* wouldn't be repeated.

Not long after, I was off on another site visit, to Banda Aceh, the capital city of Aceh province in the far northwest of Sumatra. I was particularly eager to make this visit for a couple of reasons. First and foremost, it had been the scene of enormous devastation only a couple of years earlier. A giant subterranean earthquake of 9.1 magnitude had struck just south of Sumatra, causing a humongous tidal wave to veer off in all directions in the Indian Ocean, striking any landmass in its path. Aceh was the hardest hit, with 168,000 confirmed deaths.[77]

One of our former Indonesian students from USC had been swept away by the massive wave that surprised so many Aceh residents that morning of December 26, 2004. Another friend of ours had been vacationing in southern Thailand near Phuket and had barely escaped the tsunami with his life. Emotions were still raw, both in Aceh and among those who'd lost loved ones and friends. The survivors had been left shell-shocked, even as they worked hard to rebuild their homes and workplaces.

I was also interested in seeing a part of Indonesia that was much more traditional than Jakarta in terms of its religious practices and ethnic identity. Unlike in most of Indonesia, Islamic *sharia* law was in effect in Aceh, and local morality enforcers were known to strike perceived offenders with long canes.[78] Up until the tsunami hit, Acehnese rebels, or Freedom Fighters, depending on one's perspective, had been fighting a war of independence for decades against the central government, which resulted in hundreds of thousands of displaced persons. Although Aceh had been granted political autonomy back in 1959, the Acehnese wanted to take control their oil and other natural resources.[79] In 2003, the Indonesian government had declared martial law in the province and there was a continual struggle to maintain order there. The country had other separatist movements to contend with in West Papua and the Moluccan Islands, so it didn't want to set a precedent by granting independence to Aceh.

The tsunami brought an end to Acehnese efforts to separate from Indonesia. The province's basic survival far outweighed the concerns of any political or social movements, at least in the near term. Virtually overnight, the region was gaining worldwide attention and it had become the scene of massive international relief efforts. Money poured in and the education sector soon was unexpectedly able to build new schools, provide updated computers and school materials to its students, and send faculty off to Australia, Japan, and Europe on training fellowships.

Much of this was explained to me during my site visit to a public university in Banda Aceh. I was there to visit our American fellow, Tony, who was still trying to finalize his weekly teaching schedule with his local Indonesian counterpart, Pak (the Indonesian honorific for Mister) Khairil. Two things were quickly apparent to me as I greeted the department chair and a few local staff in the English department. The display cases were full of the latest English-language teaching materials, but there were many vacant offices and cubicles, owing to the large number of faculty who had been lured away by international nongovernmental organizations to serve as interpreters or full-time staff.

Others were away on long-term sabbaticals. Some of them never returned after tasting the good life abroad. Those who remained spoke better English than their counterparts in other areas of the country, no doubt the result of interacting with relief officials involved in rebuilding Aceh.

During my visit, I observed Tony's American culture and English conversation classes. I was impressed by his efforts to elicit student reactions to a poem by Alice Walker. The settings of the poem and the classroom seemed so different at first, but upon further reflection, the themes of oppression, poverty, and hope were as relevant in Aceh as in the American South. What surprised me was the dress of his students, which was less formal and more colorful than I'd expected. The class was a mix of young male and female university students. There was no obvious segregation of the sexes at the school I visited, although apparently that wasn't the case at the religious school nearby.

The young men wore dark pants and cotton shirts, with an occasional vest or light jacket. The female students were all wearing *hijabs*, the veils that covered their necks and the tops of their heads. These accessories were a wide mix of brilliant colors, ranging from fuchsia to chartreuse. While ostensibly protecting the young ladies' modesty and shielding them from harassment, this show of colors really seemed to be emphasizing each young lady's individuality, at least from my first-time visitor's perspective. It seemed to show that even in an environment of *sharia* law, a certain amount of youthful flamboyance was tolerated.

After class, Tony, Pak Khairil and I went on a walking tour of Banda Aceh, with a special focus on how the tsunami had disrupted the life and layout of the city. As we looked out towards the beautiful harbor, Pak explained calmly that nearly all the homes and businesses along the waterfront had disappeared after the giant tidal wave had hit, crushed, and totally submerged. The town managed to fill back up with new two- and three-story constructions that were providing lodgings for the city's residents and new commercial space for entrepreneurs.

We stopped along the way at the stunning Baiturrahman Grand Mosque, which had survived the tsunami's onslaught mostly unscathed, although the neighborhood immediately nearby had been flattened. It was the only building that had remained standing in the aftermath. The city's survivors had taken heart from this, seeing it as a sign from God of what was truly important for them. As it was a Friday, crowds of men were departing from the main hall of the mosque, decked out in their prayer robes and sandals. Life appeared to have returned to normal, at least for the center city.

We continued by cab to another landmark, the Lampulo fishing boat, which is the most famous of all tsunami-related sites in Banda Aceh.[80] The locals claim that scores of residents survived the tsunami by climbing into the boat as they were being swept away by the monster tide. The boat eventually came to rest atop a house in Lampulo village, located more than a mile inland from where it had been docked when the tsunami struck. The boat remains docked exactly where it came to rest, as a testament to the brute power of nature and the whims of fate that had allowed some lucky individuals to survive.

On another visit I made to one of the well-known university towns in Central Java, I learned that one of our female fellows had been trying to cope with persistent sexual harassment by her Indonesian male counterpart. This situation is unfortunately all too common among Western female exchange program participants placed at sites where traditional male-dominated values prevail. It has negatively affected women who volunteer or do internships for international organizations such as the U.S. Peace Corps, the U.N Volunteer Program, the Fulbright English Teaching Assistants program, and many others.

In this case, the problem involved a regular pattern of verbal and physical sexual harassment that our female fellow had been suffering daily with her Indonesian male counterpart. What she described to me included unwanted touching and inappropriate invitations for coffee or meals together. The counterpart was older, married, and had a family living near the university. Our fellow was one of our most dedicated in the program and wanted to stay focused on her students. She consistently demonstrated an ability to deliver high-quality lessons in her university classes and was well liked by her colleagues. She was understandably disturbed and distracted by the unwanted attention outside of class.

During my site visit, I met with the head of the university's English department. She had taken on the role of substitute host counterpart until a decision could be made on what to do about the harasser. She expressed to me her strong concern for our fellow's welfare. She wanted to nominate a different Indonesian female candidate to serve as the local sponsor. Before passing along her recommendation to our senior program managers at the embassy, who had the final say, I attempted to track down the offending Indonesian male colleague. He'd gone home early the first day I was at the site and didn't come to the campus at all the following day.

What we were experiencing was how difficult it was to conform to non-discriminatory policies in the pairing of participating American fellows with their host-country sponsors in developing countries, where patriarchal norms still prevailed in the workplace. While gender neutrality was the goal of our American selection committee when assigning such pairings, the social and cultural expectations of American female participants and Muslim male host-country counterparts sometimes ended up miles apart, as in this case. The reality is that women of all ages are harassed in large numbers in Indonesia, just as they are in other Muslim-majority and non-Muslim countries as well. Wherever systemic sexism is embedded within the cultural norms, women become victims of such harassment through no fault of their own.

Among our female program participants, this was the only incident I learned of in which the harassment was so pronounced that it had to be documented and addressed through official channels. Our eventual decision was to remove this male educator from our exchange program. The most negative ramification for him was that he wouldn't be participating in our annual professional development workshops. I never learned whether he received any sort of reprimand from his department chair. The chances were high that he didn't. In Indonesia, more than ninety percent of sexual assault cases go unreported, as victims often fear they will be blamed for encouraging it. Some fifty-eight percent of female respondents in a national survey had experienced verbal sexual harassment. Considering these results, we were fortunate indeed that none of our other female participants[81] had reported similar incidents at their teaching sites.

———•———

During our second semester in Indonesia, Shelly arrived back in Jakarta and we were ready to get out and see the many "Big-C" cultural sights that Jakarta offered. We often headed toward the historic heart of the city along the waterfront, the area the Dutch had once called Batavia. UNESCO historians have claimed that in its heyday, no colonial town built by the Dutch East India Company came close to Batavia for its grandeur, urban planning, and architecture.[82]

As in Holland and many parts of their colonial empire, Dutch traders had constructed an impressive series of canals in their Indonesian seaports. Batavia was no exception. During the 17th and 18th centuries, Batavia serviced the largest volume of trade in the world. It was also a highly multicultural city even then. European, Chinese, Arabian, and Indian cultures met with local cultures and created a unique mixture of Pernanakan cultures. "Pernanakan" refers to cultures found in Malaysia, Singapore, and Indonesia, where Chinese and Indian immigrants married local women and thereby created highly diverse populations.

The Old Town of Jakarta, known as *Kota Tua*, has maintained some of its colonial-era facades. Our favorite stopping point was the Café Batavia, originally established in 1837. Located on the large square called *Taman Fatahillah*, the restaurant was filled to bursting with historic relics and photos from the Dutch era. I must confess that its large menu of high-quality Western fare was an especially welcome sight on our weekend visits, considering the relative scarcity of hearty, authentic Western food in much of Jakarta. This isn't to say that Jakarta didn't have many American chain restaurants and coffee shops—it certainly did. There just weren't that many elegant, European-style restaurants where you could dine in a leisurely manner while planning your day's outings.

After our meal, we generally went nearby, to either the Jakarta History Museum, called *Museum Sejarah Jakarta*, or the world-renowned Puppet Museum, called *Museum Wayang*. The History Museum is over four hundred years old and once served as the Dutch East India Company's administrative headquarters, and later, as the City Hall of Batavia. It contains an extremely eclectic collection of historical memorabilia, such as maps, weapons, ceramics and paintings that traced the city's life from its earliest times more than 1,500 years ago, through the end of the Dutch period in 1945.

The Puppet Museum was equally impressive. Shelly and I have enjoyed leather shadow puppet, or *wayang kulit*, performances in other locations, including in Bali and Thailand. There were several good specimens of these on hand at this museum. We were glad to have the chance to visit this shrine to puppetry. There was a huge collection of shadow puppets and three-dimensional wooden puppets, called *wayang golek*. Besides the many examples of traditional Javanese characters, there were also puppet displays from Thailand, Malaysia, China, India and several other countries. Colorful props, paintings, and musical instruments accompanied all of them.

Another wonderful outing, especially on weekends, was the Rangunan Zoo in south Jakarta. This zoo is the world's third oldest. The Dutch East India Company established it back in 1864. It claims to have the most diverse array of animals and plants of any similar facility worldwide.[83] Its Schmutzer Primate Center is certainly a key highlight, providing a much-needed haven for the country's endangered orangutans, as well as several chimpanzees and African gorillas. The orangutan enclosure was designed to simulate as natural an environment as possible for the animals that live there. Visitors can view them while hiking through the center, all the while invisible to the orangutans. We were struck by the human-like interaction between mother and infant orang-utans and the teen-like playfulness of the younger ones cavorting on the lawns and swinging through the trees. They reminded us of how critically important it is for humankind to preserve from extinction our nearest living mammal relatives.

———•———

Our second year in Indonesia, 2008, was a very special time to be there as Americans. Unlike the transition challenges of a year earlier in learning about this complex culture, by this time both Shelly and I had found our footing in Indonesia and were achieving a lot. We relocated further south in Jakarta, to a neighborhood called Kemang, which provided me easier access to my university campus in Depok, outside of the city.

Living in Kemang changed our perspectives entirely about the overall quality of life in Jakarta. We were suddenly living in an expatriate enclave that featured two rings of tall stone walls that provided nearly insurmountable barriers from the hustle and bustle outside. As we entered the compound, the uniformed and armed guards carefully checked our vehicle each time. If anyone was new or unknown to them, there would be questions about their reason for visiting.

It was an undeniably peaceful location. Within that first ring of walls where we lived, there existed a well-tended neighborhood with quiet streets leading to apartment buildings and a full array of townhouses and condominiums. This community, in many ways, resembled a resort, with its clubhouse, gymnasium, and swimming pool, playground, and tennis court. It reminded us of our Bangkok expatriate compound from years earlier, but on a much larger scale this time around.

Within the second ring in the same compound, there was a further checkpoint for those entering that exclusive area. There were several large well-appointed homes within that inner sanctum where high-ranking officials from the U.S. and other embassies resided, as well as members of international corporations and multilateral organizations. Because we had friends who lived there, we were able to experience the rarified atmosphere of the foreign elite of Jakarta. Shelly took advantage of following me this year to rediscover her artistic talents, participate in women's club activities, and substitute teach in art and English at a few schools, including the International School of Jakarta. She also joined me in doing outreach presentations about American culture at my two worksites at the University of Indonesia.

At work, things were going well for me. My host colleagues at U.I. and my American supervisor at the embassy were all supportive of a whole range of outreach programs intended to better inform Indonesian society about American values, democracy, and free enterprise. We were still relatively well funded, thanks to an agreement from several years earlier made by the George W. Bush administration and the Megawati Sukarnoputri government in Indonesia, to promote a stronger U.S.-Indonesia bilateral partnership through increased financial assistance.[84]

Since that agreement had been signed, the American cultural presence in Indonesia had been growing. My U.S. government-sponsored program sent ten American teaching specialists to Indonesian universities in my first year and twelve during the second. The local Fulbright Foundation, better known as the American Indonesia Exchange Foundation (AMINEF), had greatly expanded the number of English Teaching Assistants (ETAs), from just a handful in 2004 to around forty when I was there. Their mandate was to assist public and private high schools throughout the country.[85]

It also helped us enormously that a U.S. presidential candidate was considered a native son by Jakarta residents. Barack Obama had come to live in Jakarta with his mother and Indonesian stepfather in 1967, when he was five years old. Obama had lived there until age ten, attending primary school in Menteng. Many Indonesians saw his close ties with their country as a symbol of hope and religious tolerance during the U.S. Presidential elections.[86] They were closely following the U.S. primaries and took enormous pride in Obama's many victories. We met a few people who had met Obama's mother, Ann Dunham, years earlier; they spoke highly of her. She worked on rural economic development at USAID.

The timing of Obama's campaign facilitated our efforts to spread the word about U.S. democratic institutions and electoral processes. The other fellows and I made numerous presentations at American Corners, which were U.S. State Department-sponsored libraries and study areas located mostly in public universities throughout the country. Shelly and I were very proud to serve as American representatives abroad. Our feeling was very much as it had been during our time in Romania when we'd trained teachers, students, and non-profit organization officials in the fundamentals of democratic governance and civil society development.

The art and effectiveness of soft-power diplomacy, or the use of non-material capabilities, such as reputation, culture, and value appeal, to attain a state's objectives[87] never seemed more relevant to me than they did in Romania in the late 1990s, and later in Indonesia in the late 2000s. Indonesian audiences were hungry for a new social and economic model, having lived through decades of repression and stagnation linked to the iron-fisted Suharto regime. In the aftermath, the country had been transitioning for several years towards a more pluralistic and inclusive society, where peoples of all faiths could live in peaceful co-existence. Many in our audiences seemed willing to consider American policies and values as worthy of emulating.

Indonesia in that first decade of the 21st century was a fledgling democracy, in which voters still opted for candidates from well-known political dynasties, such as Megawati Sukarnoputri of the Sukarno family, or the military, men such as General Susilo Bambang Yudhoyono, but they were increasingly willing to consider outsiders. The public was frustrated by the endemic corruption that had long defined its national leadership. Indonesians finally made a breakthrough towards something truly different in their 2014 elections, when they chose President Joko Widodo, the first Indonesian leader not to come from an elite political or military background. He has been compared to Obama for his reputation as a clean politician and because of the support he received from youthful enthusiasts who called for change. He has also shown considerable empathy for the poor.

Pak Joko has been criticized for his relative lack of experience in national and international politics, just as President Obama was during his tenure in office. Time will tell if Indonesia's democracy will mature into a truly representative system of government or fall back into the authoritarian ways of the past. In recent years, the country has provided increased evidence that it is moving in the right direction, while its Southeast Asian neighbors and competitors, including Malaysia, Thailand, and the Philippines, have been sliding back into single-party domination.

———

It is sadly ironic that the very period that witnessed the peak of American soft-power diplomacy and international influence in Indonesia also featured a shocking recession. The U.S. economy declined precipitously both in 2008 and in 2009[88]. This steep downturn led to deep cuts in funding for government-supported programs that were deemed "non-essential" by America's leaders. Practically overnight, it seemed, we went from trumpeting the promising new era of President-elect Obama to devising ways public diplomacy programs such as ours could even survive.

By late 2008 and into early 2009, our program funding was cut dramatically. We went from having ample funds to having only enough to focus on our core activities: teaching American English and culture to university students. What had once been a rapidly expanding vision of an America-led, increasingly prosperous world had been transformed into a painful effort to stanch the bleeding from a serious wound. Struck from our budget were funds for such activities as developing pro-America television shows, attending conferences throughout Indonesia, and supporting lower-income Indonesian youth in gaining access to higher education.

It was a sobering time to be an American abroad. Stock markets were plummeting. Many of America's most recognized and respected companies were conducting large-scale layoffs, and some faced imminent bankruptcies. In the news, there were near-daily predictions that our country might or might not survive in the form many of us had always known and admired. This was a traumatic time of reckoning in the United States and for overseas Americans. Many wondered how our institutions could have failed us so completely. Many also questioned whether the postwar system that had served two generations was still a workable framework for the 21st century. This question has polarized our country's national dialogue ever since, and in recent years has led to a rejection by many of America's critical leadership role in the world.

———•———

Looking from our vantage point in Indonesia, it was remarkable to see an Indonesia-raised American president making strategically important decisions that managed to prevent wide-scale panic at those worst of times. There was even cause for hope amid the gloom and doom economic predictions. It still seemed possible that our country could right itself through a greater spirit of cooperation among our besieged political class. As we all know, this brighter scenario was never realized and much of our public life since then has been mean-spirited and characterized by divisiveness and inertia. It's time to try a new tack.

We're all capable of reaching out to our neighbors, both at home and abroad, for solutions that are inclusive and respectful of our many traditions, working towards a better, more peaceful country and world. The national motto of the United State describes this effort so effectively and succinctly: *E pluribus unum*—"Out of many, one."[89] Our world community today faces great challenges that can only be overcome through a united front. This was also true in American history. In 1776, thirteen colonial states declared their intent to form an indivisible nation in the face of threats to their survival. Are we today still capable of achieving such a critical accord with the stakes even higher?

Step III: Remember Our Shared Immigrant Experience

Our stays in far-flung and culturally diverse spots around the world have provided Shelly and me with an empathy towards the plight of the world's migrant populations. It's a fact of life that human migration often forces those who leave their homelands to face difficult post-arrival circumstances in foreign lands. Their early days feature an unnerving blitz of alien sights and sounds. Human history has taught us that most immigrants are adaptable enough to survive, even under these trying conditions. Eventually they manage to reinvent themselves and settle in for the long run. The ripple effect of these efforts may be felt for several generations to come.

In our own journeys, Shelly and I confronted many challenges, even though our migration was based more on a desire to experience other cultures up close than on dire economic conditions at home. Nonetheless, our early weeks in Tokyo and Bucharest were filled with hardships we could have avoided easily, by staying home in the U.S. The fact that we persisted there and elsewhere made it possible for us to learn many valuable cultural lessons. Overall, we were fortunate to have adapted successfully to vastly differing lifestyles in Japan, Thailand, Romania, Indonesia, and even Southern California.

My family history, like that of most Americans, is closely linked to the twin themes of migration and adaptation. Reflecting on my family tree, at least on my mother's side, it's clear my Irish Great-Grandfather had a very rough landing at the port of New York in 1876. He, along with millions of new Irish immigrants to the U.S., faced a daily reality of unrelenting and demeaning stereotypes, depicting them as hopeless drunkards prone to criminality.

This negative public attitude he encountered has reemerged in recent years. First-generation Mexicans and other Hispanic immigrants come face-to-face with unfair portrayals of themselves as murderers, rapists, and criminals. It's all too easy for Americans who have put down roots to point the finger of blame at newer and more vulnerable migrant populations, casting them as scapegoats for many of our social and economic troubles. Having lived through migration and bouts of cultural change during our nomadic years, Shelly and I strongly advise against succumbing to this temptation. We all need to face the fact that most immigrants have survived unthinkable threats to their well-being in their home countries and are as determined as our own ancestors ever were to create better lives for themselves in the U.S.

The classically American story of my mother's family has been a mostly positive one. Great-Grandfather Frank, whose last name was changed from "Rynne" to "Ryan" by U.S. immigration officials at the port of New York, eventually settled in Worcester, Massachusetts. He married his sweetheart Mary Ann Leonard in 1890, and by then he was working as an assembler at one the many wire works factories in that city during our country's era of rapid industrialization in the late 19th and early 20th centuries. He stayed put at the same job for over 30 years. Along the way, the couple had six daughters.

His third, named Jane, was my grandmother. She attended Teachers' College in Worcester and taught grade school for several years after World War I, before marrying Edward Cook in 1924. My grandfather

Ed was working at International Time Recording, a company that produced typewriters, time clocks, and other workplace devices. That same year, his employer renamed itself International Business Machines (IBM). The Cooks lived with their three young children in Uxbridge, Massachusetts in the late twenties before relocating in the early thirties to IBM's national headquarters in Endicott, New York. As a second-generation Irish American, my grandmother had progressed from being the daughter of a hard-working, blue-collar Irish immigrant to the wife of a white-collar businessman who, over four decades, rose to the most senior ranks of IBM Corporation.

Ed and Jane's three children, all third-generation Irish Americans, grew up shielded from the unprecedented privations of the Great Depression years that wracked our country until a period of extended warfare cranked up our country's mighty economic engine. Their second child, my mother, who was also named Jane, pursued a graduate degree at Queens College in New York in the early 1950's. She began a promising career at Proctor and Gamble Company before marrying my father, Jim Kealing, in 1953. From then onward, her vocation became defined by motherhood.

In those post World War II years, much of our country was enjoying the fever of opportunity that resulted from America's leadership of the peacetime era. For my five siblings and me, all born during the Baby Boom years of the fifties and early sixties, our cultural lineage was no longer a clear-cut line of progression as it had been for our parents and grandparents. Technically, we were fourth-generation Irish Americans on my mother's side and fifth-generation German Americans on my father's.

By the 1960s of my childhood in Kansas City, my family was seemingly rooted in the firmament of American society. Our identities as anything other than true-blue Americans seemed beyond question by that point. The reality, though, was that our cultural identities were more tenuous than we could possibly understand at the time. There was so little we knew of our family's history. Our father hardly ever spoke of his unhappy past, in which both of his parents had died at a young age. Our mother was geographically separated from her Irish-American kin, who were nearly all still living back East. For us kids, who numbered six including my older brother, Jim and sister, Karen, and younger brothers, John and Bob, and sister, Kay, only the blink of an eye, by historical standards, separated us from our ancestors who had lived far away and in very different cultures. Yet, there were few traces of these earlier generations for us as we were pursuing our modern American lifestyles shaped increasingly by prosperity and a rampant consumer culture.

I've traced my search for cultural enlightenment directly to my upbringing in Middle America at a time when many—my family included—were achieving their American dreams, in terms of the accumulation of material wealth that our ancestors could never have imagined. Curiously, at least some of us were left feeling bereft amidst the overarching sense of well-being that characterized that era of American dominance. America's Golden Age awakened in me an unmistakable restlessness to get out and experience firsthand our amazingly diverse world. Fortunately, my earliest life experiences of travel were free of the worries that plague so many of us nowadays, which enabled me to head off to points unknown without excessive worry.

Our American forbearers of earlier times could never have envisioned the world we now inhabit when they fled their homelands and risked all for the lure of a more promising life. These political and economic migrants made a conscious decision to abandon the poverty and persecutions of their old countries. Nearly all Americans have heard tales of their ancestors' bravery and fortitude. Therefore, our country's reluctance to accept the facts of its migrant origins is more than a little ironic and seems to be preventing many of us from acknowledging the undeniable interconnectedness of our country and the neighboring lands from which our own families migrated. It's well past time for a large-scale social reawakening in our land, characterized by a much greater willingness to accept and reach out to the old countries from which we Americans have sprung.

As our legacy to future generations, we should also strive to narrow the perception gaps that persist among differing peoples. We must stand ready to adapt to changing conditions as they arise. Surely the effort will be worthwhile in terms of a better, more livable world for those to come. Our hope is that these cultural portraits have provided you, the reader, with a blueprint for responding to cross-cultural challenges in your own life. We urge you to move forward as a cultural ambassador yourself.

Appendix

International Exchange Organizations
That Need Your Support

AIESEC United States
www.aiesec.org

Alliance Abroad Group (AAG)
http://www.allianceabroad.com

American Council of Young Political Leaders
http://www.acypl.org

AFS-USA: AFS Intercultural Programs USA
https://www.afsusa.org/

American Hospitality Academy
http://www.americanhospitalityacademy.com

American Immigration Council
http://www.ailf.org

The American-Scandinavian Foundation
http://www.amscan.org

AMIDEAST
http://www.amideast.org

ASSE International Student Exchange Programs
https://asse.com

CCI Greenheart
http://www.cci-exchange.org

CCUSA

http://www.ccusa.com

CIEE: Council on International Educational Exchange
https://www.ciee.org

Council for Global Immigration
http://www.acip.com

Council of International Programs, USA (CIPUSA)
https://www.cipusa.org

Cultural Exchange Network (CENET)
http://www.culturalexchangenetwork.org

Cultural Home Stay International (CHI)
https://www.chinet.org

Cultural Vistas
http://culturalvistas.org

English Language Fellow Program
https://exchanges.state.gov/us

Eurasia Foundation
www.eurasia.org/

French-American Chamber of Commerce (FACC)
http://www.faccnyc.org

The Fulbright Association
https://www.cies.org/

Institute of International Education (IIE)
https://www.iie.org

Intercultural Communication Institute
http://www.intercultural.org

Inter-Exchange Career Training USA
https://www.interexchange.org

International Cultural Exchange Organization (ICEO)
http://www.iceoinc.org

Intrax Cultural Exchange
https://www.intraxinc.com

Meridian International Center
http://www.meridian.org

Mountbatten Institute
http://www.mountbatten.org

Open Society Foundations
https://www.opensocietyfoundations.org

U.S. Peace Corps
https://www.peaceCorpss.gov

People to People International
https://www.ptpi.org

Sister Cities International (SCI)
http://www.sister-cities.org

Spirit Cultural Exchange
http://www.spiritexchange.com

Thai Community Development Center
http://www.thaicdc.org

The Ohio Program
https://ipa.osu.edu

Thunderbird School of Global Management
http://thunderbird.asu.edu

USC American Language Institute (ALI)
https://ali.usc.edu

USC International Academy
http://www.international.usc.edu

USC International Public Policy and Management Program (IPPAM)
https://priceschool.usc.edu/programs/masters/ippam/

USC Neighborhood Academic Initiative (NAI)
https://communities.usc.edu/college-access/nai/

World Learning
https://www.worldlearning.org/

REFERENCES

1 Shuler, Kurt and Bernkopf, Mark, "Who was at Bretton Woods?", Center for Financial Stability Paper in Financial History, July 1, 2014.

2 "Assessment of Member States' contributions to the United Nations", United Nations, December 28, 2016. Retrieved on August 1, 2018.

3 Experiment in International Living Website, History and Mission, Retrieved on August 2, 2018

4 CIEE 1977 Annual Report, Fulbright Norway Website, Retrieved on August 1, 2018

5 *https://www.peacecorps.gov/*, Retrieved August 2, 2018

6 Ishihara, Shintaro (1989), *The Japan that Can Say No*, New York: Simon & Schuster. Translated by Frank Baldwin.

7 Grant, Marcus and Litvak, Jorge (1998), "Drinking Patterns and their Consequences," International Center for Alcohol Policies, Philadelphia: Taylor & Francis.

8 Chowdhury, Raqib and Marlina, Roby, "Enacting English Across Borders: Critical Studies in Asia Pacific", Newcastle upon Tyne: Cambridge Scholars Publishers.

9 In person interview with Dr. Sheila Ramsey (1989), Tokyo: The International House of Japan.

10 Kealing, Jeffrey (1988), "Local Group Assists Foreign Residents of Tokyo," *City Life News*, Tokyo.

11 Hall, Edward T (1969), *The Hidden Dimension*, New York: Anchor Books.

12   Basho, Matsuo (Published in 1985), On Love and Barley: Haiku of Basho, London, Penguin Books UK.

13   Soseki, Natsume (1957), Kokoro, Tokyo: Charles E. Tuttle Publishers.

14   Machi, Tawara, Salad Anniversary, (2015) Pushkin Collection.

15   Shibusawa, Tazuko and Norton, Joy (1989), The Japan Experience, Coping and Beyond, Tokyo: The Japan Times.

16   National Capital Language Resource Center (2017), The George Washington University, An Online Teaching Resource: Washington DC.

17   Fulop, Susan (1991), Translator of Botan, Letters from Thailand, Bangkok: DK Book House.

18   Klausner, William J. (1993), Reflections on Thai Culture, Bangkok: Sayam Samakhom Publishers.

19   2010 Thailand Census, Reported by worldpopulationreview.com in 2017.

20   Bangkok Guide (1993), Bangkok: Australia-New Zealand Women's Group.

21   Chandler, Nancy, (1993), Map of Bangkok, Bangkok: nancychandler. net.

22   *http://www.dailymail.co.uk/travel/travel_news/article-3092569/ From-Frying-Pan-Lake-Flaming-Mountains-city-freezing-90-year-hottest-coldest-places-world-revealed.html* (2017).

23   *http://www.01.sil.org/lingualinks/LANGUAGELEARNING/ WaysToApproachLanguageLearning/TheNaturalApproach.htm_* (2017).

24   Hall, Edward T. (1973), The Silent Language. New York: Anchor Books.

25   About the Duang Prateep Foundation, Duang Prateep Foundation website (2017).

26   "PDA Strategies", Population and Community Development Association (PDA), Bangkok (2017).

27 *https://en.wikipedia.org/wiki/Chakri_dynasty. (2017)*

28 *http://www.u-s-history.com/pages.(2017).*

29 *http://www.npr.org/sections/itsallpolitics/2013/09/20/224530832/ not-so-fond-memories-from-the-last-government-shutdowns.*

30 *https://www.opensocietyfoundations.org* (2017).

31 *http://www.ediplomat.com/np/post_reports/prro.htm* (2005).

32 *http://news.bbc.co.uk/2/hi/europe*, 22 December 2009.

33 *https://www.theglobalist.com/fleeing-sudan-one-refugee-story*, 23 December 2015.

34 *https://www.cmu.edu/teaching/assessment/basics/formative-sum-mative.html* (2017).

35 *http://www.worldometers.info/world-population/eastern-eu-rope-population* (2017).

36 Craig S. Smith, *"Eastern Europe Struggles to Purge Security Services"*, *The New York Times*, December 12, 2006.

37 *"Hungarian minority in Romania: Hungary supporting Romania EU bid". January 18, 2005.*

38 *http://www.ijf-cij.org* (2017).

39 *https://www.simplypsychology.org/maslow.html* (2017).

40 *https://geert-hofstede.com/national-culture.html* (2017).

41 *http://www.selfawareness.org.uk/news/understanding-the-jo-hari-window-model* (2017).

42 *http://onlineslangdictionary.com/meaning-definition-of/left-coast.* (2018)

43 *http://www.latimes.com/local/education/la-me-foreign-students.* (2018)

44 Camara, Wayne J. and Schmidt, Amy Elizabeth (1999), Group Differences in Standardized Testing and Social Stratification. New York: College Board Report 99-5

45   *https://communities.usc.edu/college-access/nai.* (2017)

46   *http://www.unesco.org/new/en/unesco/themes/icts/lifelong-learning/non-formal-education.* (2017)

47   *Ardt, Kalene; Hastings, Chas; Hopkins, Katie; Knebel, Robin; Loh, Jun; Woods, Rodney (2005). "Report on Primary Education in Bangladesh: Challenges and Successes" (PDF). Rethinking International Health. Stanford University School of Medicine.* Retrieved 21 February 2012.

48   *http://articles.latimes.com/2000/jan/29.* (2017)

49   *http://thaicdc.org/ourcommunity/thai-town.* (2017)

50   *http://www.city-data.com/forum/los-angeles/146925-los-angeles-its-ethnic-enclaves-glendale.html.* (2017)

51   *http://www.theteachertoolkit.com/index.php/tool/total-physical-response-tpr.* (2017)

52   *http://www.onestopenglish.com/methodology/methodology/teaching-approaches/teaching-approaches-task-based-learning/146502. article.* (2017)

53   Yeh, Christine and Hunter, C.D. (2004), "The Socialization of Self: Understanding Shifting and Multiple Selves Across Cultures." The University of San Francisco, USF Scholarship: A Digital Repository.

54   Groode and Hatt, "Definitions of Case Study Method," *http://www. studylecturenotes.com,* (2017).

55   *http://www.npr.org/sections/thetwo-way/2013/10/30/241797346/75-years-ago-war-of-the-worlds-started-a-panic-or-did-it,* (2017).

56   *https://broadyesl.wordpress.com/2011/09/12/911-attack-victims-with-foreign-nationalities,* (2017).

57   *https://www.usnews.com/news/blogs/ken-walshs-washington/2013/04/25/george-w-bushs-bullhorn-moment.* (2017)

58   Poverty, Community-based Learning and Empowerment, UMI Dissertation Abstracts, ProQuest: Ann Arbor Michigan (2005).

59   Klausner, William J. (1993), Reflections on Thai Culture, Bangkok: Sayam Samakhom Publishers.

60   Tunsiri, Vichai (1989). Non-formal Education in Thailand: Philosophy, Concept and Practice. In Adult Education and Development: Adult Education in Thailand. Bonn: German Adult Education Association.

61   George, Pamela (1987). University Teaching Across Cultures: Lessons from U.S. Fulbrighters in Southeast Asia and Their Colleagues in Thailand. Bangkok: U.S. Information Service.

62   *http://www.sacbee.com/site-services/databases/article32679753. html*. (2017)

63   *J. Matthew Gallman* (2000), Receiving Erin's Children: Philadelphia, Liverpool, and the Irish Famine Migration, 1845-1855.

64   Worldpopulationreview.com, (2018).

65   https://www.britannica.com (2018).

66   *http://www.independent.com.uk*, "Jakarta attacks: Timeline of Indonesia's worst terror atrocities", 01/14/2016.

67   *https://www.omniglot.com*, "The Origins of Pidgin English," (2018).

68   http://*www.bbvc.co.uk* (2018).

69   *http://www.elf.georgetown.edu*, (2008).

70   http://www.ui.ac.id/page/ goal-en.htm, (2007).

71   *http://www.nwlink.com/~donclark/hrd.html* (2018).

72   Gardner, Howard (1983), Frames of Mind. New York: Basic Books, Inc.

73   http://*www.johndeweysociety.org*, (2018).

74   http://*www.worldatlas.com*, (2018).

75   http://www.news.bbc.co.uk "E.U. bans all Indonesian Airlines" (2007).

76   *https://m.imdb.com* "The Year of Living Dangerously" (1982).

77   *https://mobile.abc.net.au* "Boxing Day Tsunami: How the disaster unfolded 10 years ago" (Dec. 24, 2014).

78 Articles.latimes.com, "Aceh's morality police on the prowl for violators" (Nov. 8, 2009).

79 BBC News, "Aceh's GAM Separatists," (January 25, 2005).

80 *https://www.lonelyplanet.com*, Lampulo Boat in Banda Aceh, Indonesia (2018).

81 *https://www.reuters.com.* "Over 90 percent of rape cases go unreported in Indonesia," (July 25, 2016).

82 *http://whc.unesco.org* (2018).

83 Ninis Chairunnisa, "Ragunan Zoo Mulls Safari Night" (September 21, 2014).

84 *http://www.avalon.law.yale.edu* "U.S. and Indonesia Pledge Cooperation" (September 19, 2001).

85 *https://www.aminef.or.id/* Retrieved on August 3, 2018

86 *https://www.voanews.com*, "Obama Make Nostalgic Trip to his Indonesia Childhood Home," (June 30, 2017).

87 *http://www.internationalrelations.org*, (2018).

88 *https://www.investopiedia.com* (2018).

89 *https://www.greatseal.com.* (2018).

Images

Cover Copyright
<a href='https://www.123rf.com/profile_potowizard/ 123RF Stock Photo</a>

TOC Copyright
<a href='http//www.124rf.com/Copyright: nuvolanevicata/ 123RF Stock Photo</a>

How to Be an American Cultural Ambassador Copyright
<a href='http//www.124rf.com/Copyright: ximagination/ 123RF Stock Photo</a>

Tokyo, Bangkok, Bucharest and Jakarta Copyright
<a href='https://www.123rf.com/profile_kagenmi'>kagenmi / 123RF Stock Photo</a>

Los Angeles Copyright
<a href='https://www.123rf.com/profile_vasyll'>vasyll / 123RF Stock Photo</a>

Remember Our Shared Immigrant Experience Copyright
<a href='https://www.123rf.com/profile_usataro'>usataro / 123RF Stock Photo</a>

About the Author

Jeffrey Kealing has worked as a U.S. diplomat, professor, reporter and editor over the course of a career spent in many countries. He is a former editor at the Economist Publishing Group in New York and Tokyo, travel writer for the *City Life News* in Tokyo, and worked as a Managing Editor for *Intersect Japan* and *In Review Romania* magazines. He received his PhD in International Education from the University of Southern California in Los Angeles and has taught there as well.

To contact the author, write to him at
cultureexplorer18@gmail.com.